research in practice

Children Experiencing Domestic Violence: A Research Review

Nicky Stanley

QUALITY MARK This review has been peer-reviewed by a range of service agency directors, academics and practitioners committed to the development of evidence-informed practice. We are grateful to Helen Buckley, John Devaney, Marianne Hester, Kevin Jones, Sal Lodge, Chris McLoughlin, Kate Mulley and Viki Packman.

The author would like to thank Helen Richardson Foster who undertook the literature searches and helped with referencing and proofreading for this review. Numerous colleagues also contributed to the process of identifying and accessing relevant material; these include: John Archer, Christine Barter, Neil Blacklock, Thea Brown, Hedy Cleaver, Thangam Debbonaire, Harry Ferguson, Niki Graham-Kevan, Marianne Hester, Stephanie Houghton, Cathy Humphreys, Gillian Macdonald, Pam Miller, Lorraine Radford and Andrea Thorley-Baines.

AUTHOR'S DEDICATION For my sons, Jack and Tom

research in practice

The Granary, Dartington Hall
Totnes TQ9 6EE

e: ask@rip.org.uk

t: 01803 867692

f: 01803 868816

The full text of this review
is available on our website

www.rip.org.uk

© research in practice 2011

A CIP catalogue record is
available from the British Library

ISBN 978-1-904984-38-2 paperback

Stanley N (2011) *Children Experiencing Domestic Violence: A Research Review.*
Dartington: **research in practice**

research in practice aims to support those who work with children and families to use research in the design and delivery of services, and through this to secure better outcomes for service users. We make reliable research more accessible - summarised and interpreted with the particular needs of those working with children and families in mind. This series of research reviews addresses key issues identified by strategic planners, policy makers and practitioners. The reviews are intended to shape systems, services, approaches and practice in ways that will promote the wellbeing of children and families.

Domestic violence is a particularly pernicious and prevalent blight on childhood. Almost a quarter of young adults witnessed domestic violence as children, and we know that this will usually be repeated, not just a single episode. Separation from the perpetrator is not an effective protective: separated women are among the most vulnerable to domestic violence. Recent research on violence in young people's own intimate relationships shows what an embedded social problem this is — three quarters of girls in a relationship reported experiencing emotional violence, a third sexual violence and a quarter physical violence. Domestic violence often occurs in contexts of other disadvantage and interacts with other family problems to harm children's health and wellbeing. Cumulative exposure over time produces profoundly serious problems which can be resistant to change.

There has been much important progress in interagency collaboration over the last few years — but much more is needed. We need notification systems that are better at identifying the children most at risk, that prompt effective multi-agency intervention below the threshold for children's services, and that do not make concerns about children being taken into care a barrier to seeking help. We need services that are responsive to the needs of children and mothers particularly addressing safety, maternal mental health, parenting, helping children to recover from trauma, and building resilience in both mothers and children.

There is good evidence emerging about effective interventions, both in North America and in the UK. But the service response is still highly fragmented. The review describes a model which highlights the difference between three 'planets' — the criminal justice system and specialist services planet, the child protection planet and the planet of private law and contact. We need a new approach which engages with families on the basis of shared perceptions of harm, which seeks to involve all family members, which identifies appropriate pathways across the full range of services, which provides deep and sustained support — and above all which recognises that domestic violence is everybody's problem.

We hope this review will be of real value to those involved in commissioning and designing services; to staff working in universal, targeted and specialist settings whose roles involve identifying and supporting children and families affected by domestic violence; to staff involved in professional training and development, and across the professions engaged in safeguarding children.

Jane Lewis
Director, **research in practice**

Contents

Chapter one

Introduction

Responding effectively to children's experience of domestic violence is a major challenge for those planning and delivering children's social care services. This is in part because children's experience of domestic violence is so widespread. Chapter 2 of this review presents the latest UK prevalence figures, which show that nearly a quarter of young adults have been exposed to at least one incident of domestic violence in their lifetime (Radford et al forthcoming 2011). Subsequent to the Adoption and Children Act 2002, which defined exposure to domestic violence as a form of significant harm, children's social care departments in England and Wales have experienced a high volume of police notifications of domestic violence incidents in families with children, which has been described as overwhelming for some areas (Social Services Inspectorate of Wales 2004; Ofsted 2008; Laming 2009).

Domestic violence is deeply embedded in the pattern of family life in some communities so that victims, perpetrators and children may not recognise or define their experiences as domestic violence and this constitutes a barrier to seeking help. Moreover, it is usually a hidden experience that occurs away from public view. Bringing it out of the private sphere of the family and exposing it to wider social scrutiny can evoke shame and stigma (McGee 2000; Mullender et al 2002; Gorin 2004; Buckley et al 2007). Fears of reprisals from violent partners will also act to inhibit disclosure. Awareness of the harm domestic violence can inflict on children is increasing, but this knowledge can make parents reluctant to acknowledge that their children are living with domestic violence. Fears that social work intervention will entail children's removal into care may compound this reluctance and such fears are expressed both by parents and by children themselves (McGee 2000; Stanley et al 2010c).

While the accumulating body of evidence concerning the harmful effects of domestic violence on children's emotional well-being and development has been widely disseminated, there is much less knowledge and understanding of how children can be protected from those effects or which interventions are most successful in ending domestic violence. It is increasingly recognised that interventions that only target the victim or even those aimed at mothers and children may 'miss the mark' by omitting to engage with fathers who are the perpetrators of the most severe and frequent forms of domestic violence (see Chapter 2). This review has therefore endeavoured to maintain a focus on violent fathers despite the limited evidence regarding both their fathering and interventions directed at them.

It is difficult for both practitioners and researchers to disentangle the dynamics and effects of domestic violence on children and young people from other family problems. Chapter 2 provides evidence demonstrating how domestic violence overlaps with and can be used as an indicator for other forms of child harm. It is also closely associated with problems such as substance misuse, homelessness and mental health needs. The theme of mental health needs is woven through this review: parental mental health mediates the impact of domestic violence, and childhood experience of domestic violence contributes to mental health problems in both adolescence and adulthood. Currently, this evidence does little to shape communication and collaboration between services; this issue is considered in Chapter 8, which addresses interagency collaboration.

Many of the messages of this review concern the need for services to engage with the complex and sustained nature of domestic violence. In its most serious manifestations, domestic violence is an ongoing pattern of controlling and violent behaviour that can pervade and shape children and young people's lives. Increasingly, research is beginning to yield knowledge about interventions that can change behaviour and promote recovery. While the evidence base for many of these interventions is still in its infancy, it is possible to discern themes and patterns of delivery that characterise effective services; these are highlighted by this review.

Language and methodology for this review

It has become increasingly apparent that children's involvement in domestic violence is intimate and central rather than peripheral. This recognition is reflected by a shift in language away from children 'witnessing' domestic violence to children 'exposed to' it (Holden 2003), or 'children forced to live with intimate partner violence' (Goddard and Bedi 2010, p10). Øverlien (2010) argues for use of the term 'experiencing' as it provides a focus on the child's perspective on domestic violence; for the most part, this is the language used in this review.

There has been much debate concerning the term 'domestic violence' with some feminist groups advocating the use of the term 'violence against women' and other groups using 'interpersonal violence'. The term 'domestic abuse' is sometimes employed to ensure that non-physical forms of abuse and exploitation are encompassed. However, in the UK, 'domestic violence' remains the most commonly used term and this is the language that the wider public recognises and uses. The term 'domestic' is useful in that it emphasises that this form of harm happens primarily in the home where it is hidden from wider scrutiny. The home is the place where children and adults can expect to feel safe and secure; it should offer a haven where comfort, emotional warmth and a sense of personal control are available. For many, it is the 'last refuge': the place to retreat to when other arenas are threatening or demanding. The term 'domestic violence' juxtaposes ideas of security with images of fear and aggression and reminds us that children exposed to domestic violence experience it in a place where they have a right to feel safe.

> 'Feeling safe in homes is important because living in a house where domestic violence occurs may not feel like a real home to most people.'
>
> (Beth, quoted in Barron 2007, p16)

The definition of domestic violence adopted for this review is based on that provided by the Department of Health as, again, this is widely used in England and Wales:

> Any incident of threatening behaviour, violence or abuse (psychological, physical, sexual, financial or emotional) between adults who are or have been intimate partners or family members, regardless of gender or sexuality.
>
> (Department of Health 2005, p10)

In common with the government definition, this review has included consideration of forced marriage, female genital mutilation (FGM) and 'honour' violence. However, the review does not encompass domestic violence between family members who are not in an intimate relationship and so does not examine abuse and violence between siblings or from child to parent. While domestic violence is known to occur in same-sex relationships (Donovan and Hester 2010), there is limited evidence about how this impacts on children and the primary focus of this review is on families where adults are in heterosexual relationships. Chapter 2 considers the ways in which experience of domestic violence is gendered. While men's increasing readiness to identify themselves as victims of domestic violence is highlighted, the review acknowledges the differential impact of domestic violence on men and women by generally identifying mothers as victims or survivors of domestic violence and men/fathers as perpetrators.

There have been a number of reviews of the literature in this field undertaken by UK and Irish researchers over the last ten years, reflecting the high level of practitioner and researcher interest in the topic. Comprehensive studies by Humphreys and Mullender (2000), Hester et al (2007), Holt et al (2008) and Humphreys et al (2008) have been harnessed for this review, which attempts to build on them by incorporating research that is up-to-date and represents the latest developments in both the evidence base and service development. The time frame selected for identifying material for this review is 1995 to 2010. However, some key early studies have also been included and the review has benefited from being given pre-publication access to some recent research findings.

This review also aims to introduce a UK audience to relevant international research, particularly that from the US, Canada, Australia and New Zealand, as well as Northern Europe. While the majority of UK studies in this field are small-scale and qualitative in their approach, North American evidence is more likely to take the form of large-scale quantitative studies, which are more able to utilise control groups. This reflects different research traditions but also the levels of funding devoted to research into family violence in North America. Although the findings from some international studies may be more easily transferable to UK settings than those from elsewhere, much existing knowledge and practice in the field of domestic violence in the UK has been shaped by North American evidence and this review has sought to update this body of research and make it accessible and useful for the UK reader.

Material included in this review was identified by searching a range of on-line databases including EBSCO, Academic Search Complete, CINAHL Plus, Ejournals, PsycINFO, MedLine, Criminal Justice Abstracts and a number of others. A range of search terms were used singly and in combination with other terms, but the key ones utilised were: 'domestic violence', 'domestic abuse', 'intimate partner violence', 'family violence' and variations on these. These searches were supplemented by review of the bibliographies of key publications. In total, over 1,000 publications were identified for sorting and reading. Selection of material for inclusion has been guided by the key themes for this review with an emphasis on research evidence that has been peer reviewed. Where material is presented that is not research based, this is made explicit by employing language such as 'described' rather than the terms 'reported' or 'found', which are primarily used to present the findings of empirical research studies and reviews. In some areas where evidence is limited, information from reports produced by government or service organisations is used to fill gaps in knowledge and provide details of innovative initiatives that have not yet been evaluated.

About this review

A well-developed understanding of the extent of domestic violence and the context and circumstances in which it occurs is needed in order to appreciate the challenges that children's experience of domestic violence presents for services. Chapter 2 addresses questions of prevalence while Chapter 3 brings together the substantial body of research that has explored the effects of domestic violence on children's development. In addition to impacting on children directly, domestic violence can undermine parenting and Chapter 4 examines what is known about the interaction between domestic violence, parenting and children's health and well-being.

Recent UK research has highlighted the issue of violence in young people's intimate relationships and this is discussed in Chapter 5. Chapter 6 examines the service response to children experiencing domestic violence, exploring what is known about screening, assessment and patterns of engagement. This chapter focuses primarily on the work of children's social care, while Chapter 7 reviews evidence on the wide range of interventions delivered by other agencies. Finally, Chapter 8 considers knowledge about interagency work in this field. The conclusions and key messages of the review are presented in Chapter 9.

These chapters are connected by some questions and themes that thread through them. Crucial questions for service managers and planners concern targeting social care interventions more effectively on those who need statutory intervention, identifying models for both early intervention and for statutory services for children and families, and developing interagency collaboration in this field.

For practitioners, some of the key issues identified have included the extent to which practitioners hear and respect children's views, the needs of adolescents who may experience violence in both their own and their parents' relationships, and the challenge of engaging with violent fathers.

In some cases, the answers to these questions are emerging rather than fully formed since certain areas of the evidence base are more extensive and robust than others; for example, the evidence on the effectiveness of UK-based interventions is limited. However, the international literature in this field has expanded substantially in the last ten years and this review aims to provide a critical account that can inform the work of practitioners, managers, researchers, students and policy-makers.

Chapter two

What We Know About Children and Families Experiencing Domestic Violence

This chapter investigates:

> the prevalence of children's exposure to domestic violence in the UK

> patterns of violence within the home and family relationships

> community characteristics associated with domestic violence

> the evidence for variations in domestic violence between different ethnic groups, including the practice of specific forms of violence such as forced marriage and female genital mutilation

> parental characteristics commonly associated with domestic violence, including mental health problems, substance misuse, disability, illness, learning difficulties and homelessness

> the overlap between domestic violence and child maltreatment and its association with child deaths.

A summary of key findings is set out at the end of the chapter.

Planning and commissioning services requires an understanding of the extent of the problem. As noted in the introduction, the high prevalence of children's exposure to domestic violence represents a major challenge for the service response at both the national and local level. While much of the data on incidence and prevalence relates to adults' rather than children's experiences of domestic violence, we know that children living in households where there is ongoing domestic violence are likely to see and hear it, despite adult protestations that they were asleep at the time (McGee 2000; Mullender et al 2002; Stanley et al 2010c).

While the majority of large-scale quantitative studies in this field are based on US data, UK studies are more directly relevant for the purposes of establishing the extent of need facing those planning services in England and Wales. Where possible, this chapter draws on UK evidence but international studies have sometimes been used to fill gaps or provide comparisons. Fortunately, findings from some recent large-scale UK studies are now available to contribute to building a full picture of children and families' experience of domestic violence. We can now answer questions concerning: the prevalence of children's exposure to domestic violence; who abuses who, in what ways and when; and which families and communities are most likely to experience domestic violence. We also can explore the overlap with other forms of abuse and homicide. This chapter also addresses particular forms of domestic violence, including forced and child marriage, and identifies key contexts, such as separation and contact, where domestic violence is likely to occur.

Prevalence of children experiencing domestic violence in the UK

Understanding of the extent to which children in the UK are exposed to domestic violence has been considerably enhanced by the second NSPCC national survey on child maltreatment (Radford et al forthcoming 2011). This study surveyed three groups of children and young people: 18 to 24-year-olds and 11 to 17-year-olds responded to the survey directly, while primary caregivers responded on behalf of children under 11. Key findings from this survey of 6,195 children and young people are shown in Box 2.1.

Box 2.1: Children and young people experiencing domestic violence in the UK

	Under 11 years	11 to 17 years	18 to 24 years
Witnessed at least one type of domestic violence in last 12 months	3.3%	2.9%	12%
Witnessed at least one type of domestic violence during childhood	12%	18.4%	24.8%
Ever seen one parent kick, choke or beat up other parent (severe violence)	3.5%	4.1%	6%

(Radford et al forthcoming 2011)

This study found that childhood exposure to domestic violence was very much higher for all groups than childhood experience of the various direct forms of maltreatment. This was true even when children experiencing domestic violence were compared to those experiencing neglect in childhood, which was the most frequent form of maltreatment (childhood experience: 5% in under-11s; 12.4% in 11-17s; 16% in 18-24s). This indicates the scale of the problem that children's experience of domestic violence represents for children's services compared with other forms of child harm. While the most frequent type of domestic violence experienced entailed one parent throwing or breaking things in the context of a row, it was clear that the violence was severe for a substantial number of children and young people. Where a child or young person had seen a parent beating up another parent, men were the perpetrators in the vast majority (96%) of cases.

These figures for children's exposure to severe forms of domestic violence are comparable to those from Meltzer et al's (2009) national UK study on children and young people's mental health. Parents interviewed for this research reported that 4.3 per cent of the sample of nearly 7,865 children had witnessed severe domestic violence; this was the most frequently reported form of trauma for a child (the next most frequent was the child experiencing a serious accident). From these two recent and large-scale UK prevalence studies, we can conclude that about 4.5 per cent of children and young people in the UK are exposed to severe forms of domestic violence in their lifetime.

The Scottish Crime and Justice Survey on Partner Abuse 2008-09 (MacLeod et al 2009) measured children's exposure to domestic violence by identifying the proportion of incidents reported where children were present. A third of those experiencing partner abuse in the last 12 months had dependent children living with them at the time of the most recent/only incident and 63 per cent reported that the children were present when the abuse occurred.

There is little UK evidence available on the parenting status of perpetrators but Salisbury et al's (2009) large-scale study of the court reports completed on men convicted of a domestic violence offence in Tennessee, US, found that the majority (84.6%) of the 3,824 perpetrators had a fathering role.

Patterns of abuse

British Crime Survey (BCS) figures consistently show that domestic violence is the violent crime whose victims are most likely to experience repeat incidents: repeat victimisation accounted for two-thirds of all incidents in the 2008-09 BCS (Walker et al 2009). This means children in these families are also likely to be exposed to domestic violence on a repeated basis. In 2008-09, six per cent of women aged 16 to 59 and four per cent of men participating in the BCS reported experiencing domestic abuse (this included non-physical abuse, threats, force and sexual assault) in the past year. The BCS 2007-08 (Povey et al 2009) found that women who were separated, and women who were on their own with children, were the two groups with the highest levels of risk for all forms of domestic abuse (domestic abuse in this survey included abuse by other family members as well as that perpetrated by partners and former partners). The likelihood of being a victim of domestic abuse increased as levels of income fell and women on incomes of less than £10,000 were particularly at risk of all forms of domestic abuse. Women with a long-standing illness or disability that was described as limiting their activities were also more at risk of domestic abuse than women without long–standing illness or disabilities. Some of these findings were replicated by the National Study on Domestic Abuse in Ireland (Watson and Parsons 2005), which utilised a random telephone survey undertaken with 3,077 adults. This study also reported that risks of experiencing domestic violence were significantly higher for women with children and for women who were unemployed or prevented from working by long-standing illness or disability.

In recent years, higher proportions of men have identified themselves as victims of domestic violence perpetrated by women. This may be a consequence of increased willingness to report or it may represent over-reporting and attempts to manipulate the system; however, it also illuminates women's capacity for violent behaviour. In the US, there has been a notable increase in the rates of women arrested as perpetrators of domestic violence (Hester 2009). In some areas of England and Wales, police officers record a proportion of domestic violence incidents where both partners are identified as perpetrators (Stanley et al 2010c). This trend raises questions about the nature and severity of domestic violence and the context in which it occurs.

Hester (2009) explored issues relating to gender and domestic violence by comparing three groups of domestic violence incidents reported to Northumbria Police. These involved equal numbers of cases where women were identified as sole perpetrators of domestic violence, cases where men were the identified perpetrators and cases where both men and women had been recorded as perpetrators in separate incidents. She found that men were significantly more likely than women to use threats, harassment and physical violence while women were more likely to use weapons (at times this was in self-defence). Incidents in which men were the sole perpetrators were those most likely to produce intense fear and control of the victim. While the majority of male sole perpetrators had more than one incident on record in a six-year period, most female perpetrators had only one incident recorded.

'The Day to Count' study (Stanko 2001), which collected data on domestic violence calls to the police and other services in the UK on a single day in 2000, found that the vast majority of reports (86%) concerned female victims attacked by male perpetrators. An analysis of data on domestic violence from the 2001 BCS (Walby and Allen 2004) also throws light on the differential frequency and seriousness of domestic violence by gender. Four per cent of women and two per cent of men had experienced domestic violence (defined as non-sexual domestic threats and force) in the previous 12 months; when the definition of domestic violence was expanded to include emotional and financial abuse, these figures rose to six per cent for women and five per cent for men. Women experienced many more incidents than men: the average number of incidents for women in the last year was 20, while for men it was seven. Women were more likely to be subject to sexual assault than men. Women comprised the majority of the most heavily abused group, representing 89 per cent of those subject to four or more incidents from the perpetrator of the worst incident since they were 16. Women were very much more likely to sustain severe injuries: six per cent had sustained severe injuries in the worst incident in the last year, compared with one per cent of men. They were also more likely to describe mental health or emotional problems as a consequence of that incident: 31 per cent of women as compared to nine per cent of men did so. Box 2.2 summarises key patterns of domestic violence in the general population in the UK.

Box 2.2: Patterns of domestic violence in the general population in the UK

> Domestic violence against women is characterised by a high number of repeat incidents.

> Women who are separated, and women on their own with the children, are the groups at highest risk of experiencing domestic abuse.

> Women on low incomes are at higher risk of experiencing domestic abuse.

> Women with long-standing illness or disability are more at risk of experiencing domestic abuse.

> Both men and women can be perpetrators of domestic violence but men perpetrate more frequently and use more serious violence against women.

> Women are most likely to receive severe injuries, to experience emotional harm and to be the victims of sexual assaults.

Domestic violence and pregnancy

The Confidential Enquiries into Maternal Deaths in the United Kingdom (Lewis and Driffe 2001) estimated that 30 per cent of domestic violence started in pregnancy. However, more recent research reviews have suggested that the relationship between domestic violence and pregnancy is complex and open to debate. Jasinski's (2004) review of research on pregnancy and domestic violence found that domestic violence in pregnancy has a number of adverse consequences for the health of mothers and babies (see Chapter 3) and is associated with late take-up of antenatal care, a finding confirmed by the sixth report of the Confidential Enquiries into Maternal Deaths in the UK (Lewis 2005). However, Jasinski concludes that while hospital and clinic-based studies identify pregnancy as a time of increased risk for violence, national studies fail to show an association between pregnancy and domestic violence. She finds that most of the women abused while they were pregnant had a history of victimisation. Tallieu and Brownridge's (2010) review of international research reported that the prevalence of violence is consistently lower in pregnancy in both developed and less developed countries. They also found that violence in pregnancy was strongly associated with pre-pregnancy violence and identified a relationship between younger age and violence in pregnancy. Their review showed that violence began in pregnancy for 'a substantial minority (between 3.8% and 40.0%)' (Tallieu and Brownridge 2010). They conclude that while pregnancy offers protection for some women, it is a period of increased risk for others.

In the UK, Bowen et al's (2005) survey of 7,591 women enrolled in the Avon Longitudinal Study of Parents and Children (ALSPAC) found that fewer women reported domestic violence during pregnancy and up to two months after the birth, than did for the period 8 to 33 months post-birth. The likelihood of experiencing domestic violence increased in the post-pregnancy period. This study also found that experience of domestic violence in pregnancy was associated with a range of family adversities, including being unmarried, having a first child at an early age, low levels of education, financial problems and being in relationships characterised by substance misuse and crime.

The findings from these various studies are summarized in Box 2.3. However, what is clear is that pregnancy offers an opportunity for intervention when families' motivation to seek and utilise support is likely to be high. (The role of midwives in screening for domestic violence is discussed in Chapter 6 of this review.)

Box 2.3: Domestic violence and pregnancy

> Pregnancy offers protection for some women but increased risks for others.

> Domestic violence begins in pregnancy for a substantial minority of women.

> Domestic violence pre-pregnancy is associated with domestic violence during pregnancy.

> Domestic violence in pregnancy is associated with a range of family adversities.

> Risk of domestic violence in pregnancy is higher for younger women.

Community characteristics associated with domestic violence

Ecological analyses (Jack 2004) draw attention to the role of the environment or surrounding community in understanding child harm and in the US, the whole-community approach established in Duluth, Minnesota (Shepard and Pence 1999) provides a model for a community-focused, co-ordinated approach to domestic violence. Findings such as those from the BCS cited earlier in this chapter, which show that those on lower incomes are most at risk for domestic violence, have instigated a shift away from the view that similar rates of domestic violence occur in all communities. US studies and reviews have emphasised the links between domestic violence and neighbourhood disadvantage (Benson and Fox 2004; Herrenkohl et al 2008) as well as the association with violence outside the home (Margolin and Gordis 2000). Mitchell and Finkelhor's (2001) US study found that young people living with domestic violence and young people in households where adults were victims of other forms of violent crime had a raised likelihood of being victims of crime themselves. The risks were particularly high for girls when they lived with an adult who was the victim of domestic violence. This study suggests a relationship between community crime and violence and domestic abuse.

There is increasing UK evidence for the link between domestic violence and community disadvantage and violence. Meltzer et al (2009) found that children living in 'hard pressed' areas were over six times as likely to experience domestic violence as those in affluent areas. The BCS 2007-08 (Povey et al 2009) found that the likelihood of being a victim of domestic abuse was raised in areas where physical violence was judged to be high and for those living in rented accommodation; this survey found little variation between rural and urban areas. Likewise, the Sure Start local programmes evaluation found that higher levels of domestic abuse were discernible in two types of communities:

> well-established communities with high unemployment and a thriving business of door-to-door loan sharks

> communities where the population was much more transient, often very mixed ethnically with a large number of different languages spoken.

(Ball and Niven 2007, p11)

Men participating in Stanley et al's (2009) study of men's views and experiences of domestic violence undertaken in northern England described how their perpetration of domestic violence was interwoven with other forms of community violence encountered in childhood and with traditional and persistent conceptions of masculinity.

'I've got to be in control, got to be able to do this and I've got to be seen to be, you know, that person by others as well, I'm not being picked on ... Certainly looking at Hull, classic fishing village and stuff like that, you know, the men go out in the fishing industry and the wife's at home, the men come in, they go to the pubs, when they're back at home there's a lot of drink involved, and that side of it's dying away now but people are still here, you know, and people haven't moved on, we all still live here, you know.'

(Participant in perpetrators' focus group, quoted in Stanley et al 2009, p67)

Other parental needs

This chapter has already identified a higher prevalence of reported domestic violence in low-income families. A range of parental problems associated with domestic violence, including mental health needs, substance misuse, physical and learning disabilities and homelessness, are discussed below. These are all problems that characterise families using children's social care services and they can occur singly or in combination.

Parental mental health needs

A body of UK research provides evidence for an association between women's experience of domestic violence and a range of mental health problems. Meltzer et al (2009) found that domestic violence was associated with anxiety and depression in the parent responding to their survey; in the vast majority of cases, this was the mother. Howard et al's (2009) research review showed that studies exploring prevalence rates of domestic violence among patients with severe mental health problems identified higher lifetime rates (30-60%) than those identified by studies of the general population, with women found to have higher rates than men. A qualitative UK study (Humphreys and Thiara 2003) of women using domestic violence outreach services found an association between experience of domestic violence and suicidal behaviour, self-harm and post-traumatic stress disorder. Research with 116 mothers involved with social services reported that over half of those who were depressed and whose children were defined as 'abused' by social workers were 'living in families pervaded by abuse and violence' (Sheppard 1997, p99). The Sure Start evaluation (Ball and Niven 2007) found that mental health professionals employed by Sure Start programmes reported that domestic abuse featured in the lives of those mothers who suffered from antenatal or postnatal depression.

While most of the large-scale studies demonstrate an association rather than a causal relationship between experiences of domestic violence and women's mental health problems, qualitative studies suggest that women's mental health problems are frequently a consequence of violence or abuse they have experienced. These issues are explored further in the following chapters: Chapter 3 identifies evidence for the impact of childhood exposure to domestic violence on mental health in adulthood and discusses evidence for post-traumatic stress disporder (PTSD) in both women and children, while Chapter 4 considers how mothers' parenting is affected by mental health problems.

This review found no evidence that explored the relationship between fathers' mental health and perpetration of domestic violence. Studies of risk factors for men's perpetration of domestic violence provide evidence on their mental health but do not distinguish between men with and without children. However, US evidence (Salisbury et al 2009) suggests that the majority of men convicted of domestic violence offences will have a fathering role. A US review of research on male perpetrators (Guille 2004) notes the high levels at which personality disorders are diagnosed in this population, although she points out that this may be a product of the fact that studies are undertaken on those who are receiving psychiatric treatment. A study of the probation files of 336 convicted perpetrators in England (Gilchrist et al 2003) found that a large minority had mental health problems, with 22 per cent experiencing depression. Similarly, a meta-analysis of the risk factors associated with domestic violence (Stith et al 2004) concluded that multiple factors account for domestic violence but that depression has a moderate effect on perpetrators' physical violence. An analysis of data from the Dunedin longitudinal cohort study in New Zealand (Moffitt and Caspi 1999), which involved 861 young adults (and in some cases their partners), found that 88 per cent of perpetrators of severe domestic violence had clinically diagnosable mental health problems and 51 per cent had already been convicted of a violent crime by the age of 21.

Parental substance misuse

There is considerable evidence for an association between alcohol and domestic violence. Alcohol provides a context for domestic violence and the risk of domestic violence is increased when the perpetrator has been drinking (Downs and Miller 2002; Gilchrist et al 2003; Finney 2004; Galvani 2004). Alcohol problems also characterise perpetrators' backgrounds: a history of alcohol abuse was found in 49 per cent of the perpetrators studied by Gilchrist et al (2003). However, Galvani (2004) argues that the disinhibiting effects of alcohol do not on their own account for men's violence or negate men's responsibility for their behaviour.

While rates of drug misuse are lower than those for alcohol misuse in the general population, drug misuse is found more frequently among families involved with children's social care services (Cleaver et al forthcoming 2011). Gilchrist et al's (2003) research on perpetrators found drug misuse in 19 per cent of their sample. Humphreys et al's (2005) review suggests that perpetrators who use both drugs and alcohol are the most dangerous.

Alcohol and drug problems are also found among victims of domestic violence and this may be a consequence of their experiences of abuse (Cleaver et al forthcoming 2011; Humphreys et al 2005). In their US review, Gutierres and Van Puymbroeck (2006) note that between 41 and 80 per cent of women in substance misuse programmes reported a history of domestic violence. Miller et al's (1989) US research found that women who misused alcohol were much more likely than those in a random sample to experience domestic violence. Testa et al's (2003) longitudinal US study of nearly 1,000 women's experiences of substance misuse found that women who used hard drugs were at increased risk for domestic violence. They did not find evidence to indicate that experience of domestic violence directly influenced drug use, but they suggest that women who use drugs are likely to be in relationships with drug-using men whose lifestyles are risky and violent.

Parental disability and long-term Illness

The BCS (Povey et al 2009) and Irish studies (Watson and Parsons 2005) discussed above note a raised risk of domestic violence for women with long-standing illnesses and disabilities. Another study estimated that approximately seven per cent of women using local domestic violence services in 2006 were disabled (Hague et al 2008). A survey of domestic violence and disability agencies in North-East England (Radford et al 2006b) found that both types of organisation reported limited contact with disabled women experiencing domestic violence. Disability agencies tended to describe emotional abuse and controlling care as neglect rather than as domestic violence or abuse, while domestic violence organisations, which were frequently housed in old buildings, acknowledged that their services were often inaccessible for women with disabilities. The needs of children arising from exposure to domestic violence in these families may therefore go unrecognised.

Parental learning difficulties

While there is limited evidence concerning the actual prevalence of domestic violence among people with learning difficulties, it is known that women with learning difficulties experience high levels of violence and sexual assault generally and rates of domestic violence are likely to be high in this group of families (Sobsey 2000). Booth and Booth's (2002) study of the intimate relationships of 55 women with learning difficulties found that 22 had experienced physical or sexual violence in adult life, mainly from their partners. A re-analysis of two sets of data from studies involving parents with learning difficulties who were clients of children's social care services (Cleaver et al forthcoming 2011) found that in 42 per cent of these families there was also evidence of domestic violence and/or substance misuse. This study notes that the relationship between these factors is complex, but victims' problem drinking or drug use will in some cases be a response to domestic violence. Cleaver et al (forthcoming 2011) also suggest that mothers with learning difficulties may be those mothers who experience the most social isolation.

Homelessness

Homelessness is strongly associated with experience of domestic violence. Research with black women in London who had experienced domestic violence found that fear of homelessness acted to keep women in abusive situations and was cited by them as a reason for returning to those homes (Mama 2001). Analysis of Australian figures (Australian Institute of Health and Welfare 2005) for clients accessing the Supported Accommodation Assistance Program – the government service for homelessness – found that 33 per cent were women escaping domestic violence and 66 per cent of the accompanying children in the programme were children whose mother or carer was escaping domestic violence. Anooshian's (2005) review of the literature on homeless children found that exposure to domestic violence was a consequence of homelessness as well as a cause. She reported that homeless mothers experienced high rates of domestic violence and attributes this to the high levels of aggression in the environments frequented by homeless families, as well as women's histories of abuse, which rendered them vulnerable to further abuse. Stanley et al's (2010c) study of social services' responses to families experiencing domestic violence found that children living in homeless families were those most likely to enter the looked after system.

Ethnicity and culture

The British Crime Survey (Povey et al 2009) identified little variation in the likelihood of being a victim of domestic violence between white and non-white groups. However, this binary approach to examining the prevalence of domestic violence by ethnicity may be too simplistic. Breiding et al (2008) analysed data from the Behavioral Risk Factor Surveillance System, a random telephone survey of 70,156 men and women in ten US states, Puerto Rico and the Virgin Islands. They found considerable variation between ethnic groups in women's lifetime prevalence of domestic violence, with the highest rates reported by multiracial women and the lowest rates reported by Asian and Hispanic women. Other large-scale studies undertaken in the US, New Zealand and Canada (Field and Caetano 2004; Marie et al 2008; Brownridge 2008) show differential levels of risk among different ethnic groups.

The National Study on Domestic Abuse in Ireland (Watson and Parsons 2005) collected useful data on Traveller women and children through analysis of refuge figures and three focus groups held with Traveller women. Traveller women accompanied by children were found to represent 45 per cent of all refuge admissions in 2003 (this high figure may reflect the absence of other resources available to Traveller women); they were more likely to be accompanied by children and more likely to have more children than settled women. Traveller women participating in the focus groups described a tradition of Traveller men exerting social and financial control over their partners and suggested that women were more exposed to violence now that more families lived in settled accommodation where they were less open to the scrutiny of the wider Traveller community.

The study also found that the risk of severe domestic violence was substantially higher for women born outside Ireland (24% of women born outside Ireland experienced severe domestic abuse in their lifetime compared with 14% of women born in Ireland) and for women whose partners were born outside Ireland (25% compared to 10% in their lifetime and 13% compared to 4% in the previous five years). Most of the immigrant women and men included in this survey were European.

Forced marriage

As noted in the introduction (see Chapter 1), government guidance includes forced marriage in its definition of domestic violence, although as Chantler et al (2009) note, this definition applies to adults only. Forced marriage is distinguished from arranged marriages (which both participants freely consent to) and is defined as occurring:

> where one or both parties are coerced into a marriage against their will and under duress.
>
> (Foreign and Commonwealth Office et al 2006)

The Forced Marriage (Civil Protection) Act 2007 prohibits the practice, inducing or aiding of forced marriage and makes provision for protection orders prohibiting the acts that precede a forced marriage. Forced marriage usually involves marriage to someone who lives abroad and plans to settle in the UK and the age at which a person from outside the European Union can be sponsored as, or can enter the UK as, a spouse has now been raised to 21 (Chantler et al 2009). However, Chantler et al's (2009) study found no evidence that this had impacted on the incidence of forced marriage. Gill and Mitra-Khan (2010) argue that in England and Wales forced marriage has been framed as an immigration and border control problem rather than being conceptualised as violence against women.

Child marriage, which is marriage before the age of 16, has been defined as a form of forced marriage and it may be characterised by a lack of free and informed consent (Gangoli et al 2009). In 2009, 33 per cent of victims in cases in which the Forced Marriage Unit provided assistance were under 18 years of age and 14 per cent were under 16 (DCSF News 2009). While government guidance (HM Government 2010) directs that forced marriage involving children should automatically be handled as a child protection issue, professionals responding to Kazimirski et al's (2009) study of forced marriage reported that children's services were unwilling to engage with cases involving 16 and 17-year-olds who had no disability or other mental health problems. The study identifies 'a gap' in the response to this group, which may reflect the wider confusion that surrounds marriage in this group in England and Wales where young people aged 16 to 18 are permitted to marry with parental consent (Gangoli et al 2009).

The hidden nature of forced marriage has made it difficult to determine its extent in the UK. By bringing together data from a questionnaire distributed across ten local authorities and data from national organisations, Kazimirski et al (2009) estimated a prevalence of between 5,000 and 8,000 reported cases in England. They found that within the local organisations surveyed, 96 per cent of reported cases concerned female victims and 41 per cent involved victims under 18. Ninety-seven per cent of those seeking help from local organisations were Asian; this contrasted somewhat with 2008 figures from the Forced Marriage Unit, which reported that 64 per cent of cases concerned Pakistani victims, 15 per cent were Bangladeshi, 8 per cent were Indian, while the remaining 14 per cent comprised families from a range of ethnic groups (Kazimirski et al 2009). This focus on South Asian groups is likely to reflect the remits of the local organisations and the Forced Marriage Unit.

A mapping survey of voluntary and statutory organisations (Chantler et al 2009) found that while South Asian communities were most frequently cited as those in which forced marriages took place, respondents also identified forced marriages happening in Somalian and other African communities, Chinese, Middle Eastern and South American groups, as well as some East European communities. The study also included interviews with survivors of forced marriage who identified an association between forced marriage and poverty, with marriage being viewed as a means of securing financial security for the bride's family. Forced marriage was also seen as a device for restricting 'deviant' sexuality or enforcing sexual propriety and the researchers found that this form of control and surveillance could continue into the marriage and beyond it. A case study in Luton (Khanum 2008) also identifies forced marriage as a starting place for domestic violence. Domestic violence can be described as associated with forced marriage in three key ways:

> Forced marriage is in itself a form of domestic violence where the perpetrators are usually family members.

> Those participating in forced marriages may be children themselves: in this sense, forced marriage is abusive in exposing them to a range of adult experiences and life changes to which they have not freely consented.

> The coercion implicit in forced marriages may be a feature of the marriage itself and any children may be exposed to domestic abuse and violence.

Female genital mutilation

Female genital mutilation (FGM) is defined both as a form of domestic abuse (Department of Health 2005) and as a child protection issue (HM Government 2010). Carrying out, aiding, abetting, procuring any form of FGM has been an offence in the UK since 1985 and the Female Genital Mutilation Act 2003 made it an offence for FGM to be performed on a UK national or permanent resident anywhere, so ensuring that girls cannot be taken abroad for FGM to be performed. Dorkenoo et al (2007) undertook a study to estimate its prevalence in England and Wales using updated figures from the 2001 census to estimate the population size of UK groups from countries where FGM is widely practised. The largest population groups in the UK from FGM-practising countries were those from Ghana, Kenya, Nigeria, Somalia and Uganda. The highest estimated numbers of women with FGM were from Kenya and Somalia. The prevalence of births to women with FGM increased between 2001 and 2004 and was found to be particularly high in inner London (6.3%) and outer London (4.6%), with high rates also identified in other UK cities such as Liverpool, Birmingham, Sheffield and Cardiff. The researchers estimated that 24,012 girls under 15 were at risk or may have already experienced FGM, with six to eight years being the most common age for FGM in countries where the prevalence is high. This study identified a range of harmful consequences for girls and women, including restricted mobility and barriers to urination, menstruation, sexual intercourse and giving birth, as well as psychological consequences.

Separation, contact and abduction

There is substantial UK evidence that domestic violence continues beyond separation and may be exacerbated by it. As noted above, the BCS (Povey et al 2009) identified women who are separated as among those most vulnerable to domestic violence. A study of 251 domestic violence incidents notified by the police to children's social care in England (Stanley et al 2010b) found that in 54 per cent of cases the couple were separated. The post-separation period represents a time of especially high risk. Richards's (2004) analysis of multiagency domestic violence murder reviews in London found that women were particularly at risk of homicide in the first two months following separation. She reviewed 241 cases of domestic sexual assault reported to the police in London and discovered that half the couples in her sample were in the process of separating or had separated. Her study also highlighted that in ten per cent of cases children were reported as witnessing the sexual assault.

Contact and access to children provide a setting where domestic violence regularly erupts, thereby ensuring that children are intimately involved. The 2001 BCS reported that where women continued to see their former partner because of the children, this contact resulted in threats, abuse and violence in over a third of cases (Walby and Allen 2004). Radford and Hester (2006) found the vast majority of women (94% and 92%) participating in their two studies of contact arrangements reported being abused post-separation in the context of contact. Stanley et al (2010d) found that 19 per cent of domestic violence incidents took place in the context of contact, and issues relating to child contact featured in 30 per cent of the incidents studied by Hester (2009).

A study of post-separation violence (Humphreys and Thiara 2003) found it continued to be a problem for longer for the black and minority ethnic (BME) women participating in their research. For South Asian women, post-separation contact may be particularly risky since it may re-connect them with members of the extended family who may have been implicated in abuse previously or may assert ownership of the children (Thiara 2010).

Estimates vary concerning the proportion of family proceedings cases where domestic violence is a significant factor. The review conducted by Cafcass and Her Majesty's Courts Service (HMICA 2005) noted that a range of estimates 'up to 70% and above' could be identified.

Domestic violence is also associated with child abduction, both in cases where the perpetrator of domestic violence takes the children and in cases where victims, usually women, flee from domestic violence taking the children with them (Shetty and Edleson 2005). A US survey (Hegar and Greif 1991) found that over half (54%) of abductions involved domestic violence. A study of abduction in California (Johnston et al 2000) reported that mothers who abducted were more likely to be the victims of abuse, while fathers who abducted were more likely to be perpetrators. Shetty and Edleson (2005) examined cases of children abducted across international boundaries that were dealt with under the law established by the Hague Convention 1980. They found that about a third of the cases (identified through online legal databases) included a reference to some form of family violence; 70 per cent of these included details of domestic violence. They argue that the Hague Convention should be amended to include exposure to domestic violence as a valid form of 'grave risk', which is the criterion that provides an exception to the principle that a child should be returned to his or her habitual residence.

Overlap between domestic violence and child maltreatment

Domestic violence has been recognised as a key indicator for child abuse and neglect. A review of 35 North American studies found an overlap ranging from 30 to 60 per cent between domestic violence and child maltreatment in families where either form of abuse was identified (Edleson 1999b). Appel and Holden's (1998) research review found high rates in the region of 40 per cent for the co-occurrence of domestic violence and physical child abuse when studies focused on populations of abused women or abused children. However, they noted fluctuating rates across studies, particularly among those that used community samples; they suggested that for the general US population a co-occurrence figure of six per cent was more accurate.

In the UK, the NSPCC prevalence study (Radford et al forthcoming 2011) undertaken with a sample of the general population found that young people experiencing family violence were between 2.9 and 4.4 times more likely to experience physical violence and neglect from a caregiver than those young people not exposed to family violence. Similarly, Moffitt and Caspi's (2003) New Zealand study found that children's risk of abuse was three to nine times higher in homes where parents fought one another than for other children in their study.

A number of UK studies undertaken in the 1990s examined the overlap between domestic violence and child maltreatment in police or social work caseloads. One study examined referrals to police child protection and domestic violence units in one police force (Browne and Hamilton 1999) and found an overlap of 21.6 per cent; however, 46.3 per cent of child protection files indicated domestic violence in the family. In over half (59%) of the 29 child protection cases of physical abuse, neglect and emotional abuse studied by Farmer and Owen (1995) there was concurrent domestic violence, while domestic violence was evident in two-fifths of the sexual abuse cases. A study of social services cases (Brandon et al 1999) identified domestic violence in 47 per cent of families where children were assessed as experiencing or likely to experience significant harm.

Some US studies have explored the relationship between children's experience of domestic violence and neglect. Hartley (2004) studied a sample of 159 confirmed cases of child maltreatment that occurred in Iowa between 1995 and 1998 and compared cases where the assessments found no domestic violence, less-severe domestic violence and severe domestic violence. She found that neglect involving denial of critical care and lack of supervision was most likely to be the sole form of maltreatment in those families with the most severe forms of domestic violence. A larger study that examined all 2,350 cases of child neglect investigated by Child Protective Services in Kentucky, US, in 1999 found that domestic violence was recorded in 29 per cent of cases (Antle et al 2007). Children in families where domestic violence and neglect overlapped were more likely to have problems in cognitive and interpersonal functioning than those in families where only neglect was reported. In common with Hartley's findings, the types of neglect most frequently associated with domestic violence were lack of safety, a lack of supervision, emotional neglect and refusal of treatment such as mental health services. The co-existence of domestic violence and neglect was also associated with a lack of social support.

A telephone survey of 1,149 mothers in Carolina, US (Chang et al 2008) explored the relationship between domestic violence and child maltreatment, distinguishing between families where both partners were perpetrators and those where only one parent was, and between different forms of domestic violence and different forms of child maltreatment. The study found that partner psychological abuse increased the likelihood of child neglect, particularly when the perpetrator of that abuse was the man. Psychological abuse between parents also increased children's risks of maltreatment generally, with children most likely to experience emotional abuse when both parents were involved in partner psychological abuse and most likely to experience physical abuse when the man was responsible for psychological abuse of the mother.

Domestic violence has also been found to be associated with child sexual abuse. Research in the US with 179 mothers and their children recruited from domestic violence shelters and from the community (half of whom had experienced domestic violence) found an association between domestic violence and children's experience of sexual abuse (McCloskey and Bailey 2000); this was determined through interviews both with mothers and children themselves. However, regression analysis identified maternal sexual abuse history, together with maternal substance misuse, as the strongest indicator of child sexual abuse. A study of 164 children and young people attending a sexual abuse clinic in Texas found that 52 per cent lived in households characterised by domestic violence (Kellog and Menard 2003). In the UK, a study of the case files of an NSPCC team (Hester and Pearson 1998) found that over half the sexual abuse cases involved domestic violence and that the perpetrator of sexual abuse was most likely to be the child's father or father figure when domestic violence was also evident.

Animal abuse

Cruelty to animals has been identified as a useful indicator of both domestic violence and child abuse, although attempts to establish these links have aroused some controversy (see Piper and Myers 2006; Becker and French 2006). Becker and French's (2004) review reported that animal abuse could occur in the context of domestic violence and could be used to intimidate children. They found that the links between animal cruelty, domestic violence and child maltreatment were complex and required further research but argued that there was sufficient evidence to merit the development of links and dialogue in the form of a cross-reporting protocol between those agencies concerned with animal welfare and those concerned with children's welfare. A retrospective survey of 860 students from three Mid-West and West US states (DeGue and DiLillo 2009) provided further evidence for an association between animal abuse, domestic violence and child abuse. Students who reported witnessing or perpetrating animal abuse were more likely to have a history of child maltreatment or have been exposed to domestic violence, suggesting that animal abuse could provide a useful indicator for both domestic violence and child maltreatment.

Association with child deaths and femicide

Domestic violence has consistently been identified as a feature of serious case reviews (SCRs) into child deaths in England and Wales (Reder et al 1993; Reder and Duncan 1999; Sinclair and Bullock 2002; Rose and Barnes 2008). An overview of SCRs in England identifies high levels of domestic violence in the cases studied (Brandon et al 2009). Domestic violence was the most frequently mentioned parental characteristic in all 189 SCRs reviewed, while in-depth study of 40 case reviews from 2006-07 revealed that over half the children were living with past or present domestic violence, which was often found in combination with parental mental health problems and substance misuse.

Saunders (2004) reviewed the deaths of 29 children in 13 families who were killed as a consequence of contact arrangements between 1994 and 2004 in England and Wales. She found that domestic violence was a feature in 11 of the 13 families. In five cases, the killings appeared to have been conceptualised as a form of revenge on the children's mother.

Domestic violence provides the most common context for femicide in the UK with most deaths occurring in the period after a woman leaves her partner (Povey 2004). In the US and Canada, Domestic Violence Death Review Committees (DVDRCs) review deaths that occur in the context of domestic violence. Jaffe and Juodis (2006) provide an overview of reports from 14 DVDRCs and identify a range of ways in which children were victimised by domestic homicides:

> children were left without parents

> children were exposed to their parent's violent death

> children were indirectly killed as a result of attempting to protect a parent or were 'caught in the cross-fire'

> children were directly killed by a parent in an act of revenge against their partner

> children were indirectly/directly killed as part of a murder-suicide plan directed against the family

> adolescents were killed as a result of violence in their intimate relationships.

Children were affected by the domestic homicides in between 35 and 65 per cent of cases reviewed by the DVDRCs included in this study.

'Honour' killings are an extreme form of domestic violence where perpetrators seek to legitimate acts of homicide on the grounds that expressions of female sexuality reflect on the family and community's sense of honour and shame. As Meetoo and Mirza (2007) note, these concepts of honour and shame act to restrict access to support for women who are victims of domestic violence, leaving them isolated within their own communities and in wider society. HM Government (2010) quotes an estimated figure of 12 'honour' killings per year in England and Wales. The UK Honour Network hotline, which was established in 2008, received over 2,000 calls in its first six months (Afzal 2009).

Chapter two: Summary

> Recent UK prevalence studies indicate that about 4.5 per cent of children and young people have experienced severe forms of domestic violence in their lifetime.

> Children and their mothers are likely to experience domestic violence on a repeated basis.

> Women who are separated and on their own with children are the groups most at risk of all forms of domestic abuse.

> Men are more frequent perpetrators of domestic violence and use more serious violence against women who are more likely to experience serious harm.

> There is limited UK evidence on rates of domestic violence for different ethnic groups but rates are likely to be highest in communities where traditional patriarchal attitudes and roles persist.

> Families on low incomes and mothers with long-standing disabilities or illness are more likely to experience all forms of domestic abuse.

> Domestic violence begins in pregnancy for a substantial minority of women but is also associated with pre-pregnancy violence. It is more likely in pregnancy for younger women.

> Domestic violence is associated with disadvantaged communities where levels of crime and other forms of violence are high.

> Research has identified a strong association between mothers' experience of domestic violence and their mental health problems, particularly depression. There has been less research undertaken on the mental health of fathers who perpetrate domestic violence.

> The risk of domestic violence increases when the perpetrator has been drinking and alcohol problems characterise the history of perpetrators. Drug misuse problems are generally high among families using children's social care services. Women may develop substance misuse problems in response to their experiences of domestic violence.

> Homelessness may be both a consequence of domestic violence and a means by which children are exposed to it.

> Forced marriage is defined as a form of domestic abuse in itself, but children can also be participants in forced marriages and the coercion that distinguishes the act of forced marriage may continue into the marriage and affect children.

> Female genital mutilation (FGM) is illegal and is defined as a form of domestic violence in England and Wales. Girls from FGM-practising countries such as Ghana, Kenya, Nigeria, Somalia and Uganda are most at risk.

> Domestic violence continues beyond the point of separation for approximately half of all families and the post-separation period has been identified as a particularly high-risk time.

> Contact provides a context in which domestic violence can be perpetuated. Domestic violence is also associated with child abduction.

> Domestic violence is a key indicator for child abuse and neglect. In the general UK population, children and young people experiencing domestic violence are between 3 and 4.5 times more likely also to experience physical violence and neglect. Domestic violence has also been found to co-exist with child sexual abuse.

> The concurrence of domestic violence and child abuse and neglect is high in children's services' caseloads where research identifies an overlap in about 50 per cent of cases. In the context of child protection cases, domestic violence is frequently found to co-exist with neglect involving lack of supervision or refusal of treatment.

> Animal abuse has been identified as an indicator of both domestic violence and child abuse and researchers have argued for cross-referral mechanisms between professionals employed in animal welfare and those in child protection.

> Domestic violence is associated with child deaths and characterises a high proportion of families who are the subject of SCRs.

Chapter three

The Impact of Domestic Violence on Children and Young People

This chapter considers what is known about the nature of children's experience of domestic violence and its impact on their development and behaviour. Specifically, it examines the evidence relating to:

> the mechanisms whereby domestic violence affects children's health and development, including the emotional impact, the effects of secrecy and stigma, the consequences of trying to care for an abused parent, and neurobiological evidence for the impact on brain development

> the impact of domestic violence on children at different stages of their development – in infancy, during school years, in adolescence – and on into adulthood

> resilience and the factors that help to protect children and young people, including personal characteristics, family characteristics and sources of support within the community, including friendships

> the risk factors associated with worse outcomes for children, including poor maternal mental health, parental substance misuse, family displacement and poly-victimisation, which includes children's exposure to both domestic violence and child abuse.

A summary of key findings is set out at the end of the chapter.

Decisions about intervention in families where children are experiencing domestic violence need to be informed by an understanding of how exposure to domestic violence impacts on children, in both the short and long term. There is now a considerable body of research, mainly from North America, that identifies and measures the effects of living with domestic violence on children's behaviour and development and a number of reviews and meta-analyses synthesise findings from such studies (Edleson 1999a; Kitzmann et al 2003; Onyskiw 2003; Wolfe et al 2003; Fowler and Chanmugam 2007; Holt et al 2008; Chan and Yeung 2009). However, examining the impact of domestic violence on children is not straightforward and those undertaking reviews (Edleson 1999a; Holt et al 2008) have identified the key challenges for research in this field. They note the need to distinguish between the effects of exposure to domestic violence and other forms of child abuse or neglect, as well as the concern that early research was heavily reliant on data collected from women and children in refuges, who were not necessarily representative of those experiencing domestic violence in the wider population. Moreover, much research has relied on mothers' accounts of both domestic violence and its impact on children. This may have coloured the evidence: Chan and Yeung's (2009) meta-analysis found that ratings of the adjustment problems of children experiencing domestic violence varied according to which group of informants was reporting.

As noted already, a corollary of this emphasis on mothers is that research into perpetrators of domestic violence as fathers is as yet very limited. The previous chapter identified an absence of evidence concerning the mental health of abusive fathers and how that might contribute to children's vulnerability. Research that captures children's perspectives is also limited. Many of the larger-scale North American studies that have collected data directly from children focus on measuring psychopathology rather than exploring their views or experiences. UK and Irish qualitative studies that privilege children's own accounts (McGee 2000; Mullender et al 2002; Buckley et al 2007), and which bring together the perspectives of survivors, perpetrators and children (Stanley et al 2010c), can provide evidence that explains the processes that underpin the outcomes measured by large-scale surveys and clinical studies.

The nature of children's experience of domestic violence

Although parents may struggle to acknowledge the extent of children's exposure to domestic violence, it is unlikely that children will be unaware of violence and abuse that is severe and ongoing. The previous chapter noted that Scottish crime figures for 2008-09 (MacLeod et al 2009) showed that children were present in 63 per cent of all reported domestic violence incidents, while a study of domestic violence incidents notified to children's services in England (Stanley et al 2010d) found that 61 per cent of children directly witnessed the incident. Mullender et al's (2002) UK research emphasised the extent to which children and young people assumed active roles in coping with domestic violence, protecting their mothers and siblings and seeking help at the time of the incident. Likewise, nearly a quarter of mothers participating in a telephone survey of 114 abused mothers in four US cities (Edleson et al 2003) found that children intervened physically in domestic violence. Over half the mothers surveyed reported that their children would occasionally, frequently or very frequently yell at the abusive man while in the room where violence was happening. The previous chapter noted that many domestic violence incidents reported to the police occur in the context of men's contact with their children. An account of such an incident taken from police records indicates how children may experience such an event:

> A man stood outside the family home yelling at his former partner, who would not let him in as he was drunk. He claimed he was there to give money to his son. He smashed his way into the home, continuing to yell at the woman and threw money at his son. The 9-year-old son barricaded himself and his mother in the bedroom.

> (Incident cited in Stanley et al 2010c, p102)

Arguments about disciplining children can also form the backdrop to incidents (Stanley et al 2010c) and some of the early US literature on domestic violence confirms the ways in which conflicts about child rearing can act as triggers for violence (Straus et al 1980). Further research with children and young people could usefully explore the extent to which they perceive themselves to be implicated in domestic violence and how this perception affects them.

Emotional or psychological abuse that is woven into family interactions and communications is also difficult for children to escape and may result in a home environment dominated by fear, control and the anticipation of violence.

Taxonomies of exposure

Holden (2003) has developed a taxonomy of exposure which he argues could be used to further understanding of variations in children's responses to the experience of domestic violence. What this taxonomy lacks, however, is any consideration of a time element – exposure to an isolated incident is clearly a different experience from regular exposure. The taxonomy shown in Table 3.1 also focuses on physical assault and fails to take account of the abusive emotional climate within a household where children regularly observe their mother being insulted, denigrated and controlled by her partner.

Table 3.1: Taxonomy of children's exposure to domestic violence (DV)

Exposure Type	Definition	Examples
Exposed prenatally	Real or imagined effects of DV on the developing fetus	Fetus assaulted in utero; pregnant mother lived in terror; mothers perceived that the DV during pregnancy had affected their fetus
Intervenes	The child verbally or physically attempts to stop the assault	Asks parents to stop; attempts to defend mother
Victimised	The child is verbally or physically assaulted during an incident	Child intentionally injured, accidentally hit by a thrown object etc
Participates	The child is forced or 'voluntarily' joins in the assaults	Coerced to participate; used as spy; joins in taunting mother
Eyewitness	The child directly observes the assault	Watches assault or is present to hear verbal abuse
Overhears	The child hears, though does not see the assault	Hears yelling, threats or breaking of objects
Observes the initial effects	The child sees some of the immediate consequences of the assault	Sees bruises or injuries; police; ambulance; damaged property; intense emotions
Experiences the aftermath	The child faces changes in his/her life as a consequence of the assault	Experiences maternal depression; change in parenting; separation from father; relocation
Hears about it	The child is told or overhears conversations about the assault	Learns of the assault from mother, sibling, relative or someone else
Ostensibly unaware	The child does not know of the assault, according to the source	Assault occurred away from home or while children were away; or occurred when mother believed child was asleep

(Holden 2003, p152)

McGee (1997) provides a similar analysis that does incorporate an abusive emotional climate. She identifies the following six types of exposure:

> children physically present during the violence

> children overhearing the violence

> children witnessing the outcome of the assault

> use of the child to intimidate the mother

> children as triggers of violence

> children aware of the emotional and psychological abuse.

Both these taxonomies have their limitations, but they could be adapted to provide a useful tool to open up the extent of children's exposure to domestic violence with parents. As is the case with other forms of child harm, practitioners may struggle to develop a clear picture of the severity and extent of children's exposure to domestic violence. Using these taxonomies to explore the nature of exposure might also offer the opportunity to examine issues of severity and extent.

Direct injury to children

Children's intimate involvement in domestic violence means they risk being injured themselves, particularly if they intervene to protect their mothers. One study described the injuries seen over a period of ten years in children presenting at the emergency department of Philadelphia Children's Hospital following incidents of domestic violence (Christian et al 1997). In 40 of the 139 (29%) cases for which medical records were studied, children were injured when held in a parent's arms and 33 (24%) children and young people were injured when attempting to intervene. Younger children were more likely to sustain head or facial injuries. A study of 68 young children (median age nine months) with non-accidental head injuries who presented at a South African hospital over a period of three years found that nearly half (47%) were described as not the intended victim (Fieggen et al 2004). Some of the injuries sustained, such as knife injuries, suggested that the children had been intentionally or unintentionally used as a shield. The figures for direct injuries to children are much lower when non-clinical populations are studied. A UK study of 251 incidents of domestic violence incidents reported to the police (Stanley et al 2010c) found only three cases where children were injured, although in a number of other cases children were pushed, dragged or hit.

As noted in Chapter 2, there is debate about whether pregnancy increases the risk of women experiencing domestic violence (Jasinski 2004); however, there is clear evidence about the impact of physical assault in pregnancy on the unborn child. A large-scale survey of nearly 15,000 young Australian women aged 18 to 23 (Taft et al 2004) identified a strong association between experience of partner violence and both miscarriage and termination. Jasinski's (2004) review identifies a number of studies that show an association between domestic abuse and miscarriage or spontaneous abortion, while a study undertaken in Seattle found that the risk of pre-term births and neo-natal deaths was significantly associated with reports of domestic violence in pregnancy (Lipsky et al 2003). Low birth-weight may also be associated with the experience of domestic violence in pregnancy (Boy and Salihu 2004; Sarkar 2008), although Rosen et al (2007) note that, while domestic violence was a risk factor for low birth-weight infants in their sample of 148 women, low birth-weights were most likely to be found when women were also experiencing depression, post-traumatic stress disorder and/or poor diet.

A review exploring the impact of domestic violence on children with disabilities found no strong evidence for an association between domestic violence in pregnancy and children born with disabilities (Baldry et al 2006).

Impact of exposure to domestic violence on children's health and development

Understanding the mechanisms

UK and Irish research (Mullender et al 2002; Buckley et al 2006) which forefronts children's accounts tends to emphasise the high levels of fear and anxiety experienced by children exposed to domestic violence:

> '... I have to sleep watching two doors and with my back against the wall.'
>
> (12-year-old white girl, quoted in Mullender et al 2002, p111)

Children's accounts also highlight the extent to which the anticipation of violence infuses their lives with the tension resulting from unpredictability. An analysis of calls to ChildLine (Saunders et al 1995) reported children's accounts of 'walking on eggshells'. This participant in McGee's (2000) research described a state of being constantly on the alert:

> 'Constantly on edge. Never free, never safe. It was like, there was no safe [place] ... being at home wasn't safe at all, it was just that's the place where you are and you're constantly alert. You don't sleep properly, you just sit there and wait for something to happen.'
>
> (Mona, aged 17, quoted in McGee 2000, p72)

Anxiety about others is another aspect of this state of constant alert or hypervigilance. A US comparison of two groups of children, one of which had been exposed to domestic violence while the other had not (Graham-Bermann 1996), found that children who had experienced domestic violence were significantly more worried about the vulnerability of their mothers and siblings than those in the comparison group.

Studies undertaken from the perspectives of children and young people also draw attention to the effects of the secrecy and stigma surrounding domestic violence on young people's self-confidence, self-esteem and consequent capacity for making relationships with peers (McGee 2000; Gorin 2004). One young person participating in Buckley et al's (2006) Irish study described the feelings of stigma and isolation experienced in relation to other children:

> 'I felt that I had a neon sign that told everyone what was going on in my family ... I felt that I wasn't on the same wavelength as people. When I was small I used to run to school and I used to feel like I was on a different wavelength from them and I thought that I was not normal in comparison to the rest of them ... I thought that they were all happy families or whatever and I was kind of like the outcast. And plus you're bottling up your feelings and you kind of feel very alone.'
>
> (Young person, quoted in Buckley et al 2006, p38)

Feelings of anger and resentment are also described by young people. Young people in Stanley et al's (2010c) study described their own anger and aggression and that of their siblings as a product of their exposure to their parents' violence:

> 'Just angry and then like you'll take it out on your mum and things, it's been building up and then it's just war at them, and then they think that you don't care about them because you shout at them.'

> (Tremayne, participant in young people's focus group, quoted in Stanley et al 2010c, p26)

Children and young people may take on caring tasks and responsibilities when their mothers are experiencing domestic violence (Gorin 2004; Cleaver et al forthcoming 2011). While young carers may find their role provides self-esteem and satisfaction, it may also be a source of worry and act to isolate them from their peers and distract them from schoolwork (Becker et al 1998). Like the young participants in Buckley et al's (2006) research, young people in Stanley et al's (2010c) study communicated some resentment about being forced to 'grow up' and to assume adult responsibilities in order for their families and themselves to 'survive':

> 'You have to grow up quicker because if you didn't then you'd just, you'd melt, you'd just go.'

> (Jodie, participant in young people's focus group, quoted in Stanley et al 2010c, p27)

In contrast to the social perspective adopted by UK research, US research has tended to make more frequent use of diagnostic categories: research reviews consistently find high rates of both internalising behaviours (sadness, withdrawal and anxiety) and externalising behaviours (aggressive and antisocial) in children who have experienced domestic violence (Onyskiw 2003; Fowler and Changmugam 2007). US research is also more likely to harness the concepts of trauma and post-traumatic stress disorder (PTSD), which clinical researchers identify in both victims of domestic violence and their children. For instance, research with 50 mothers and children who had experienced domestic violence found high rates of PTSD in both groups – although, interestingly, PTSD in children was not associated with PTSD in their mothers (Chemtob and Carlson 2004). The authors note that mothers with PTSD were less likely to seek help for their children than other mothers in their sample. Similarly, an Australian study (Mertin and Mohr 2002) of 56 children aged 8 to 16, whose mothers had recently been living in domestic violence shelters, found that 20 per cent met the diagnostic criteria for PTSD.

Graham-Bermann and Levendosky (1998) reported that over half the 64 children in their sample of 7 to 12-year-old children who had experienced domestic violence in the last year exhibited intrusive trauma stress symptoms, nearly a fifth were experiencing trauma symptoms involving avoidance or repression of thoughts related to the violence, and just under a fifth displayed traumatic arousal symptoms such as sleep problems or difficulties in concentration. However, only 13 per cent of the sample qualified for a full clinical diagnosis of PTSD. A later study (Graham-Bermann and Seng 2005) of 160 pre-school children recruited through Head Start programmes found that children's health problems, such as asthma, allergies and ADHD, were associated with exposure to domestic violence and that traumatic stress reactions predicted their health independently of other experiences. A study of PTSD in a sample of 8 to 17-year-olds attending community mental health clinics in New York (Luthra et al 2009) found that exposure to domestic violence was one of the forms of interpersonal trauma significantly associated with a diagnosis of PTSD.

Developments in neurobiology (Teicher et al 2002) have identified the mechanisms through which adverse environmental experiences such as domestic violence can impact on brain development. Saltzman et al (2005) found higher levels of salivary cortisol and elevated heart rates indicating heightened physiological arousal in children exposed to domestic violence. This chimes with children's accounts of being constantly alert, waiting for something to happen. Cummings et al (2009) describe a programme of longitudinal research that aims to identify the ways in which experience of domestic violence affects the neurobiological systems, so influencing children's adjustment. In their model, exposure to domestic violence triggers activity in the sympathetic and parasympathetic nervous systems, which, they suggest, together regulate arousal, affect and attention in children.

What factors make for harmful outcomes?

In the absence of evidence of direct injury inflicted on children, practitioners and managers making difficult decisions about safeguarding will be keen to know which factors are likely to indicate harmful outcomes for children. Given that over a third of children exposed to domestic violence do not appear to do any worse than other children in the community (Kitzmann et al 2003), it would be helpful if research was able to provide answers about which children exposed to domestic violence are likely to fare worst. Unfortunately, the evidence is far from conclusive. This is partly because research suffers from problems similar to those that practitioners face – that is, domestic violence is not easy to observe and measure. Attempts to synthesise findings from a range of studies, particularly the large-scale studies using validated measures favoured by US researchers, struggle with the lack of a common definition that is specific about matters such as the extent of children's exposure to domestic violence and the nature of the abuse. Since studies may be examining a wide range of experiences, clear findings often fail to emerge from meta-analyses. For example, although some studies (Evans et al 2008) have suggested that the impact of exposure to domestic violence may differ for boys and girls, a quantitative meta-analysis undertaken across 118 studies (Kitzmann et al 2003) found no strong evidence that gender or age had a substantial influence in moderating the effects of exposure to domestic violence. Wolfe et al's (2003) meta-analysis and Fowler and Chanmugam's (2007) review of five meta- and mega-analyses produced similar findings.

For practitioners, it would be helpful to have evidence concerning the cumulative effects of exposure to domestic violence. There is evidence from one study of children in the community (Graham-Bermann et al 2009) that the amount of violence a child is exposed to in a year is significantly associated with his or her level of adjustment. However, this review identified few longitudinal studies that examine the long-term effects of differing levels of exposure to domestic violence. Rossman's (2000) US study is important in this respect and is described in Box 3.1.

Box 3.1 Impact of exposure to domestic violence over time

Research Methods

The sample included 176 children and their mothers recruited from both community settings and shelters. The research distinguished between child participants according to the extent to which they had been exposed to domestic violence in their lifetime. Thirty-six per cent (n=63) of this group were followed up over a period of 11 months.

Findings

> Children's PTSD symptoms and behavioural problems were significantly worse for those children who had had the longest lifetime exposure to domestic violence.

> Maternal ratings of PTSD symptoms for children with higher levels of exposure to domestic violence showed significant improvement over the 11-month follow-up period. This drop was particularly noticeable when children had received treatment.

> Mothers' ratings of their children's school performance reduced over the same period when violence was ongoing.

Conclusion

Rossman argues that treatment is associated with better outcomes and that ongoing violence in some families during the follow-up period explained the decline in school performance. This study provides considerable support for an accumulative model of adversity for children exposed to domestic violence: repeated exposure over time produces worse outcomes. It was not the case that children became habituated to domestic violence and showed fewer negative responses to it over time.

(Rossman 2000)

These findings support Wolak and Finkelhor's (1998) argument that chronic exposure to domestic violence over time will produce serious problems that are more resistant to intervention. However, while ending children's exposure to domestic violence as soon as possible is clearly a priority, the evidence reviewed in Chapter 2 makes it clear that violence often continues beyond the point of separation.

Differential impact by developmental stage

Infancy and pre-school children

While research reviews do not consistently demonstrate worse or better outcomes for particular age groups exposed to domestic violence, the research does suggest that the effects may be manifested differently for differing age groups. The evidence for the impact of domestic violence on infants and pre-school children comes primarily from US studies undertaken by clinicians; there is little UK research addressing the impact of domestic violence on this age group. Studies have identified delayed language and toilet-training, sleep disturbance, emotional distress and a fear of being left alone in infants and toddlers (Osofsky 2003; Lundy and Grossman 2005). Bogat et al (2006) used mothers' reports to explore infants' responses to domestic violence and found that 44 per cent of infants exposed to one incident of domestic violence showed at least one trauma symptom – that is, increased arousal, numbing or aggression. This study found that infants were most likely to show symptoms of trauma when their mothers also showed such symptoms. Chapter 7 of this review includes an example of an intervention designed specifically for mothers and their babies.

Pre-school children have been identified as the group exhibiting most problems (Levendosky et al 2003), which include aggressive behaviour, temper tantrums, sleep disturbance, anxiety and despondency (Cunningham and Baker 2004; Lundy and Grossman 2005; Martin 2002). A US study of 100 three to five-year-olds (Huth-Bocks et al 2001) found poorer verbal abilities in the 43 per cent exposed to domestic violence in the last year. The vulnerability of pre-school children to a range of adverse effects may result from a combination of accumulated exposure to domestic violence throughout their lives, together with limited capacity to escape it or manage it intellectually, verbally or emotionally.

School-age children

A UK survey examining the impact of domestic violence on the mental health of school-age children and young people (Meltzer et al 2009) found that witnessing domestic violence was significantly associated with conduct disorders in children. Bream and Buchanan (2003) also provide useful findings from a study undertaken in England and Wales that examined the emotional health of school-age children who were subjects of welfare reports for the court following parental divorce or separation. A history of domestic violence was strongly associated with children receiving borderline or abnormal scores on the Goodman Strengths and Difficulties Questionnaire (SDQ), which was completed by parents.

The young people participating in Buckley et al's (2007) Irish study were anxious about keeping their home situation a secret and about the possibility of being bullied at school; they described difficulties in concentration and problems with attainment. However, school could represent a 'safe place' for some children (Buckley et al 2007, p303). A small-scale study with 12 educational professionals in Northern Ireland (Byrne and Taylor 2007) elicited descriptions of children exposed to domestic violence as being either quiet and withdrawn or loud and aggressive in school settings.

The impact of exposure to domestic violence may account for some of the emotional and behavioural difficulties of children in the looked after system. A UK study of 68 looked after children and young people (Farmer 2006) found that 52 per cent of the sample had a history of experiencing domestic violence in their birth families, while Moyers et al (2006) found that a pattern of earlier adversity, which included exposure to domestic violence, made it more likely that children and young people had contact with someone rated as detrimental to them. Similarly, an Australian study of 364 children with high levels of placement instability found that experience of domestic violence before entering out-of-home care characterised nearly three-quarters of the sample, together with histories of physical abuse and parental substance misuse (Osborn et al 2008). Interventions with looked after children need to address their experience of domestic violence, and contact and reunification plans should take on board the possibility of ongoing domestic violence in children's birth families.

Adolescence

As young people attain adolescence, their responses to living with domestic violence are more likely to attract a mental health diagnosis or a label of delinquency. A large-scale survey of nearly 4,000 American adolescents found that anger was the most evident trauma symptom in young people exposed to domestic violence (Song et al 1998). A longitudinal US study of 296 women and their children that followed the children through to adolescence (McCloskey and Lichter 2003) found that exposure to domestic violence was associated with aggression towards peers. It was also associated with depression in adolescence, which was found to be particularly prevalent among girls in the sample. Young people's experience of domestic violence was also found to be correlated with their aggression towards a parent, usually the mother.

In their study with Scottish schoolchildren aged 11 to 17, Alexander et al (2005) reported that when young people were asked to identify the feelings that would characterise young people living with domestic violence, those who were currently experiencing domestic violence at home described feelings of fear, sadness and loneliness, including suicidal feelings. In contrast, their peers who were not experiencing domestic violence attributed predominantly angry feelings to children living in such situations. A study of 140 adolescents in Dublin who had been identified as at high risk for mental health problems through screening in school discovered that the 14 young people who reported psychotic symptoms in face-to-face interviews were ten times more likely to have experienced domestic violence than those without such symptoms (Kelleher et al 2008a).

Experience of domestic violence is also associated with delinquency in adolescence. The UK NSPCC prevalence survey (Fisher 2011) found that exposure to domestic violence was significantly related to delinquency in adolescent girls.

Impact in adulthood

Various studies (Silvern et al 1995 in Edleson 1999a, Howells and Rosenbaum 2008) have linked depression in adult life to childhood experience of domestic violence. A large-scale survey using face-to-face interviews with 3,023 adults in Paris found an association between childhood exposure to domestic violence and recent depression in adulthood; this continued to be significant even when the analysis allowed for the effects of family and social stressors (Roustit et al 2009). Similarly, Russell et al's (2010) research involving a random sample of 1,205 young adults showed an association between frequent childhood exposure to domestic violence and depressive symptoms, which was maintained even when experience of other forms of childhood abuse was accounted for.

Violent behaviour and tolerance of violence in intimate relationships can be carried into adult relationships (Edleson 1999a). A large-scale US study (Whitfield et al 2003) found that the risks of being a perpetrator or victim of domestic violence were significantly greater for those who had experienced domestic violence as children. Another US study of 1,099 adult male perpetrators of domestic violence (Murrell et al 2007) found that those who witnessed domestic violence as children committed domestic violence most frequently as adults. Similarly, Murrell et al's (2005) earlier paper explored the use of weapons in domestic violence and found that perpetrators who reported having witnessed their parents threatening to use (or using) weapons were more likely to replicate such behaviour in their own relationships.

Resilience

A quantitative meta-analysis of studies that compared adjustment problems in children known to have been exposed to domestic violence with community samples (Kitzmann et al 2003) showed that about 63 per cent of those who had experienced domestic violence had worse outcomes than children in the community samples. However, as the authors note, this finding also indicates that over a third of children who had experienced domestic violence were doing at least as well as other children in the community. Most of the studies described above which used a clinical diagnosis of PTSD as an indicator of harm found that this diagnosis was applicable to only a minority of children exposed to domestic violence. A US study of 175 eight to 16-year-olds receiving support from a community programme for children experiencing domestic violence (Spilsbury et al 2008) used psychological assessments to divide participants into three clusters representing children's patterns of adjustment. The largest cluster (69%) consisted of children who did not reach the threshold for a clinical diagnosis. Given such findings, some authors (Edleson 1999a) have argued that exposure to domestic violence should not be defined as a form of child maltreatment or abuse. This is questionable however; arguably, the definition in English and Welsh legislation of children witnessing domestic violence as a potential form of significant harm has done much to alert professionals to its harmful effects for children. There are also questions about where the cut-off point for children's social care intervention should be fixed. Nevertheless, it is clear that exposure to domestic violence does not invariably result in substantial harm to children's health or development. Understanding which factors make for resilience and distinguish those children who will not experience adverse effects is key to targeting resources effectively (Edleson 2004).

Resilience can be understood as including the resources that can protect children from the experience of domestic violence, facilitate adaptation and promote recovery (Margolin 2005). However, Jaffee et al (2007) define resilience as achieving normal development in the face of considerable adversity. These varying definitions exemplify the confusion as to whether resilience is a process, a goal or a characteristic of an individual child (Graham-Bermann et al 2009). The question of when a child's resilience is assessed is important, as development may be affected at different stages and in varying ways. Collishaw et al (2007) characterise resilience as 'an ongoing process of developing the competencies necessary to form, maintain and benefit from supportive relationships'. Perhaps because resilient children are less likely to come to the attention of services, research has tended to focus on identifying and exploring risk factors for children's exposure to domestic violence. Less is therefore known about what makes for resilience that is specific to children's experiences of domestic violence. However, it is possible to extrapolate from some of the studies that examine children's resilience to all forms of maltreatment.

Resilience factors intrinsic to the child

Rutter (1985) provided an early account of the key characteristics that promote resilience in the individual child:

> a sense of self-esteem and confidence

> a belief in one's self-efficacy

> a repertoire of problem-solving approaches.

Evidence to support Rutter's model is provided by a US study, which classified 228 children aged 8 to 18 living in domestic violence shelters into five clusters representing different levels of adjustment (Grych et al 2000). Those children for whom no problems were reported evinced significantly less self-blame than children in the clusters defined as multiproblem or mild distress, suggesting the importance of a capacity to attribute negative experiences externally. Graham-Bermann et al (2009) undertook a similar study in a community context by investigating levels of adjustment in 219 children aged 6 to 12 who were receiving community services following experience of domestic violence. Twenty per cent of the sample were identified as resilient and this cluster was characterised by high levels of self-worth and social competence. Offering children and young people opportunities to participate in activities that develop confidence and confirm self-esteem can therefore be identified as a route to building resilience and Chapter 7 describes some interventions that aim to achieve this.

High IQ has been identified as a resilience factor for children experiencing maltreatment. A longitudinal twin study involving 1,116 families in England and Wales (Jaffee et al 2007) used home visits and teachers' assessments of children at the ages of five and seven to establish levels of antisocial behaviour. They found that high IQ functioned as a resilience factor for boys who had experienced maltreatment before the age of five, but it was not significant for girls.

Resilience in the family

Various reviews (Osofsky 2003, Holt et al 2008) have highlighted a supportive relationship with a caring adult as the key protective factor for children experiencing domestic violence. This figure is often the mother, as emphasised by Mullender et al's (2002) UK research with children. Gerwitz and Edleson (2007) argue that interventions aimed at protecting children from domestic violence should focus on promoting mother-child attachments. Other supportive adults, such as grandparents, aunts or older siblings, can also offer supportive relationships that convey continuity, security and a sense of being loved.

Ghate and Hazel (2002) point out that resilience in the family can be reinforced by the ways in which services are delivered. Their survey of 1,754 parents living in deprived parts of Great Britain found that parents valued services that allowed them to retain a sense of efficacy and personal control. A sense of self-worth is an important component of resilience for parents as well as children:

> 'Support' means that you are still in charge, the parent is still in charge and you are asking for help, advice and whatever – but you are the one in charge. You are not handing over your kids to someone else to take over.'
>
> (A mother – a lone parent – living on a low income with a sick child, quoted in Ghate and Hazel 2002, p26)

Sources of resilience in the community

Social support has been identified as a key factor that can protect children from the impact of parental problems. Jaffee et al's (2007) UK study found that resilience in children who had been maltreated before the age of five was associated with living in low-crime neighbourhoods with high levels of social cohesion. Booth and Booth (1998) found that resilience in families where parents had learning difficulties was fostered by participation in the wider community; this could be achieved through children being in mainstream schooling, parents' jobs, membership of local clubs and organisations, or close-knit neighbourhoods. In the US context, Cox et al (2003) found the risk of maltreatment was reduced for children who also experienced domestic violence when their mother attended church regularly, indicating involvement with local religious groups.

Daniel and Wassell's (2002) review of the literature on resilience emphasises an association between children and young people's friendships and resilience. Friendships can promote self-esteem but the type of friend matters: in adolescence, friendships with young people involved in offending can lead to delinquent behaviour. Studies that have elicited children's views (McGee 2000; Mullender et al 2002; Gorin 2004) emphasise that friends are often one of the first sources of support and the people to whom children confide experiences of domestic violence. However, children and young people describe taking care to ensure that those friends they talked to can be trusted to respect their confidentiality and take them seriously. Daniel and Wassell (2002) argue that social workers need to pay more attention to children and young people's friendships and Chapter 5 of this review considers how friends' views may impact on young people experiencing violence in their own intimate relationships.

Risks

Mothers' mental health

As noted above, US research has tended to focus on mothers' mental health as a key factor mediating the impact of children's exposure to domestic violence at the expense of any consideration of fathers' mental health. However, it makes sense that while a supportive relationship with their mother can protect children, the lack of a supportive relationship will increase the likelihood of adverse effects. Mothers who have severe mental health needs of their own (often as a consequence of experiencing domestic violence) may struggle to provide children with consistent care and a sense of security. Chapter 2 highlighted that mothers' mental health needs are frequently associated with domestic violence. In the US, Dubowitz et al (2001) studied the impact of both abuse in childhood and domestic violence on mothers' mental health and their children's behaviour, health and development. The sample comprised 419 mothers and their children who were already receiving health services and were described as a 'high risk'; mothers reported on their own and their children's health using validated measures when the children were aged four to five years and at six years. The researchers found evidence to support Rutter's (1989) model of cumulative risk: those mothers who had experienced both childhood abuse and domestic violence were the most depressed, were most likely to use harsher forms of parenting and reported the most behavioural problems in their children.

An Australian study collected data on 60 pre-school children of 46 mothers who had recently left abusive partners and were living in short-term accommodation (Zerk and Mertin 2009). Children's behavioural, emotional and social functioning was found to be associated with their mothers' levels of parenting stress, rather than with the levels of violence experienced. The most frequently reported symptoms in children were increased arousal, fears and aggression, distress on separation, poor concentration and sleep problems, all of which the researchers identified as post-trauma symptoms. The researchers argue that mothers' high levels of emotional distress, which were related to the levels of violence they reported, impinged on their parenting, which in turn impacted on the children. However, this study (like others exploring the relationship of these factors) relied heavily on mothers' reports of children's behaviour, so findings concerning children's symptomatology may be an artefact attributable to their mothers' perceptions.

It is useful, therefore, to find that these results are reinforced by a US study that drew on a number of sources of evidence to assess children's outcomes. English et al's (2003) research is described in Box 3.2.

Box 3.2: Factors impacting on children's health and behaviour in families involved with child protection services

Aim

To examine the relationship between domestic violence and children's health and behaviour in families involved with child protection services.

Research methods

The sample included 238 children referred to child protection services. Interviews were completed with both mothers and children, and data from child protection services records and teachers' assessments of children's behaviour were collected. Children were assessed at ages four and six.

Findings

The severity and frequency of domestic violence in these families was found to have no direct impact on children's health and behaviour at the age of six. Instead, levels of domestic violence were closely associated with caregiver and family functioning, which included the caregiver's depression and general levels of hostile and aggressive behaviour in the family. This, in turn, impacted on children's health and behaviour at the age of six.

(English et al 2003)

While UK studies (see Chapter 2) have consistently identified an association between mothers' experiences of domestic violence and mental health problems, particularly depression, this review did not identify any large-scale UK empirical studies that have systematically explored the relationship between domestic violence, mothers' mental health and children's behaviour or mental health.

Substance misuse

The previous chapter noted the strong association between alcohol and domestic violence and Leonard's (2001) review found that where they co-exist, domestic violence is likely to be more frequent and the injuries sustained more serious. Velleman et al (2008) completed interviews with 45 young people from five European countries whose parents were affected by alcohol problems and compared them with a small comparison sample of 12 young people whose parents did not have alcohol problems. Rates of psychological and physical aggression (both father to mother, and mother to father) as well as parental injuries from domestic violence were very much higher for parents with alcohol problems. Parents who had alcohol problems also used more extreme forms of violence against their children, while fathers with alcohol problems were reported to be more violent to children than mothers with alcohol problems. Over a third of the young people affected by parental alcohol problems were assessed as reaching borderline or clinical levels of behavioural and emotional problems.

Cleaver et al's (forthcoming 2011) review emphasises that the risks of poor outcomes for children increase when they experience both parental substance misuse and domestic violence. Her study (Cleaver et al 2007) of initial assessments undertaken on 267 children's social care cases in England found that those families for whom there was evidence both of domestic violence and substance misuse, were those where children were most likely to have developmental needs; where parenting capacity was most likely to be severely affected; and where there were most likely to be severe difficulties in relation to family and environmental factors. The review (Cleaver et al forthcoming 2011) stresses the importance of establishing the nature and extent of substance misuse, but notes that high levels of substance misuse will impact on a family's living standards and may involve parents in criminal activities such as shoplifting, drug dealing or prostitution. This may expose children to additional forms of violence or inappropriate sexual activity (Barnard 2007).

A UK study of social work intervention with London families characterised by parental misuse of drugs or alcohol (Forrester and Harwin 2008) found that domestic violence was one of the factors associated with the poorest outcomes for children. Children experiencing domestic violence in addition to substance misuse were also less likely to be taken into care than other children. The authors suggest that the threat of violence led to more tentative social work intervention with these families and they argue for practitioners to consider initiating care proceedings when substance misuse and domestic violence combine with a lack of co-operation in families.

Parents and children with disabilities

The previous chapter noted that the risk of domestic violence is raised for women with disabilities and long-term illnesses. Parental learning difficulties, as well as mental illness and substance misuse, have been identified as a strong predictor of adverse outcomes for children who are also experiencing domestic violence (Cleaver et al 2010). High rates of abuse have been identified among children with disabilities (Westcott and Jones 1999; Sullivan and Knutson 2000) and have been attributed to their isolation, communication difficulties and the stigma associated with disability. These factors may also make them particularly vulnerable to exposure to domestic violence. However, there is little research that specifically addresses disabled children's experiences of domestic violence. Baldry et al's (2006) review indicated that practitioners may lack the skills needed to facilitate disclosure of domestic violence by children with communication difficulties. They suggest that practitioners may confuse children's responses to domestic violence with the effects of autism or interpret such responses as challenging behaviour associated with a disability.

Other concurrent forms of child harm

Edleson's (1999a) review found worse outcomes for those children who had both been exposed to domestic violence and had been the direct target of abuse themselves. Likewise, a research review examining the co-occurrence of physical abuse and exposure to domestic violence (Herrenkohl et al 2008) found compelling evidence of overlap between the two. The authors argue there is sufficient evidence to conclude that the two forms of abuse together have a compounding 'double whammy' effect on the mental health of young people and adults. A study involving face-to-face interviews with 152 African American mothers and their children (Kaslow and Thompson 2008) found higher rates of psychological distress in those children who had experienced child maltreatment and whose mothers reported severe levels of physical violence. A US study of 37 young children with sexual behaviour problems (Silovsky and Niec 2002) found that while most did not have substantiated histories of sexual abuse, over two-thirds had been exposed to domestic violence or domestic violence and physical abuse (see Chapter 2 for studies that have examined the prevalence of experience of domestic violence in children receiving treatment following sexual abuse).

Finkelhor's large body of US research (Finkelhor et al 2005; Finkelhor et al 2007a; Finkelhor et al 2007b; Finkelhor et al 2009b) has moved increasingly towards a focus on poly-victimisation. He argues that the children at highest risk of adverse psychological effects are those who are exposed to a range of forms of abuse, including exposure to domestic violence, bullying, property crime and violence in their intimate relationships, as well as to various forms of child maltreatment. Finkelhor et al (2009a) analysed data from a telephone survey of nearly 1,500 respondents, which entailed interviews both with children (where they were over nine years of age) and caregivers. They found that a calculation of the lifetime inventory of the full range of vicimisations could, when additional weight was given to child maltreatment and sexual assault, predict the level of psychological disturbance for a child. However, they suggest that calculating poly-victimisation over the last two years may provide a more accurate picture of the immediate risks.

Dislocation

Dislocation is often a consequence of the decision to end an abusive relationship. Stafford et al's (2007) study with 30 young people in Scotland found that relocation following separation resulted in peer and friendship difficulties (see also Buckley et al 2007). These young people also described a range of losses consequent on relocation, including loss of home, possessions and pets, as well as relationships with the extended family. In some cases, relocation can involve separation from siblings (McGee 2000; Mullender et al 2002). A Kidspeak online consultation (Barron 2007) on domestic violence invited children and young people to post comments on both open and closed-access online message boards. While some of the 105 children and young people who responded were positive about the opportunities refuges afforded for moving on and making new friends, others resented the losses and restrictions imposed by the move to a refuge.

'my dad was mean to my mum, me, my sister - he never let me go out and hang with my friends - when I went in a refuge my life was ruined because I could not have friends round - my sister blamed every thing on me - I wanted to go home and when I went to my dads he didn't want me - I was too much to handle me when I dint do noffing wrong.'

(Ellie aged ten, quoted in Barron 2007, p17 - punctuation added)

Øverlien (2011) interviewed 22 children and young people in Norwegian refuges and found that the need to keep their location a secret resulted in confusion and complicated relationships with peers. Confusion could be exacerbated by a failure to explain to children where they were or why they were there. Assisting mothers to provide children with explanations about why they are in a refuge and the need for secrecy should be identified as a key task for refuge staff.

Chapter three: Summary

> Children's involvement in domestic violence is intimate and active. A minority will experience direct physical injury. Taxonomies of children's exposure to domestic violence offer a useful structure for exploring the nature of children's involvement.

> Qualitative research with children and young people has identified a range of emotional and behavioural responses to the experience of domestic violence; these include fear, anxiety, worry, stigma and isolation, caring responsibilities and accompanying resentment, anger and aggression.

> US research undertaken in clinical settings has classified these responses as internalising and externalising behaviours, and has increasingly focused on the identification of post-traumatic stress disorder (PTSD), although this is found at the level of clinical diagnosis in a minority of most samples. Increasingly, neurobiology is offering accounts of how exposure to domestic violence triggers responses in the nervous system, which impact on arousal mechanisms in children.

> Not all children suffer adverse effects in response to exposure to domestic violence. Estimates vary as to what proportion will experience harm but there is evidence to support theories that the impact of exposure is cumulative and that longer exposure produces the most severe impact.

> The impact of domestic violence on children differs by developmental stage: infants and pre-school children show delayed development, sleep disturbance, temper tantrums and distress; schoolchildren experience conduct disorders, problems in concentration and difficulties with peers; while adolescents display depression, delinquency and aggression towards peers.

> Experience of domestic violence characterises the history of a substantial proportion of looked after children. Contact and reunification plans need to include consideration of ongoing domestic violence in birth families.

> Childhood experience of domestic violence is associated with depression in adult life and the likelihood of being an adult perpetrator or victim of domestic violence increases for those who experience domestic violence as children.

> Resilience to the effects of domestic violence is associated with a child's individual, family and community characteristics. At the individual level, self-esteem and self-efficacy, which can involve external attribution of responsibility for adverse events, are important. At the family level, the availability of an adult (usually the mother) who provides a consistent supportive relationship contributes to resilience. At the community level, friendships can offer children and young people social support.

> Mothers' mental health problems have been identified as a key factor that may increase the likelihood of harm for children exposed to mental health problems. A context of parental substance misuse also increases the risk of poor outcomes for children and the criminal lifestyle associated with drug misuse particularly may expose them to additional risks.

> When children experience domestic violence in addition to other forms of abuse and neglect there is a high risk of psychological harm.

> Dislocation frequently occurs when women and children leave abusive households; this can result in confusion and multiple losses for children. Children need explanations for such disruption and refuge staff should assist mothers to provide this.

Chapter four

Domestic Violence and Parenting

This chapter examines the evidence for the impact of domestic violence on children through its effect on parenting and parenting capacity. This includes discussion of:

> the evidence base relating to the effects of domestic violence on mothers' parenting, including increased maternal mental health needs and substance misuse, the importance of community and social support, and the capacity for mothers' parenting to recover from the effects of violence

> what is known about abusive men's parenting and their relationships with their children, including their understanding of the impact of their violent behaviour on the children

> the evidence relating to children's experience of domestic violence in the context of post-separation contact, including evidence for perpetrators' use of contact as a means of perpetuating violence and control

> a hierarchy of priorities that could be used to inform decisions about contact.

A summary of key findings is set out at the end of the chapter.

The previous chapter explored the impact of domestic violence on children and young people and identified the ways in which exposure to domestic violence can compromise their mental health, behaviour and development. This review has also noted the protection from adverse effects afforded by a child's strong supportive relationship with his or her mother and conversely, the risks represented by poor mental health in mothers. This chapter considers whether and how domestic violence can impact on children through the way in which it undermines parenting. Since previous research has often focused exclusively on mothers, the parenting of both mothers and fathers is considered here.

Unpicking the direct effects of experiencing domestic violence from those that can be attributed to parenting in the context of domestic violence represents a challenge for research. Moreover, domestic violence impacts on more than just parenting skills: it can have the effect of uprooting women and children from their homes and neighbourhoods, thereby severing supportive ties with friends, extended family, school and workplaces. It can prove difficult to discriminate between the impact of these losses and that of particular parenting skills or styles, since parenting may change in a new setting where familiar supports are no longer to hand. Furthermore, research that relies on mothers' accounts of their own parenting may be influenced by mothers' perceptions, which may be coloured by depression or by attempts to portray themselves as 'good parents' when under scrutiny (Levendosky et al 2003). Practitioners face similar challenges in attempting to assess parenting in families experiencing domestic violence.

Mothering in the context of domestic violence

Research that has aimed to explore the impact of domestic violence on mothers' parenting has delivered a variety of messages, not all of which are consistent. Earlier studies (Holden et al 1998; Sullivan et al 2000) tended to conclude that the parenting of mothers who had experienced domestic violence could be maintained in the face of domestic violence. However, more recent studies have emphasised that while the quality of mothers' parenting can be diminished in the context of domestic violence, it can recover in its absence.

There are various mechanisms through which mothers' parenting can be undermined by abusive partners. Mothers may internalise humiliating and undermining messages from their partners – 'You're a useless mother' – and lose confidence in their parenting skills. Abusive men may seek to disrupt the mother-child relationship, forge alliances with children against their mother and encourage children to question their mothers' authority (Bancroft and Silverman 2002); in this sense, the abuse can be seen to target a mother's identity and functioning as a mother. Thiara (2010) draws on a number of her UK studies to suggest that a key aspect of abuse experienced by South Asian women is the perpetrator's denial of the mother's relationship with her children and his collusion with his parents and siblings to reinforce this message. A study of domestic violence within South Asian communities, which analysed accounts from service providers together with calls made to the NSPCC's helpline services (Izzidien 2008), also identifies this pattern of abuse, which acts to sever mothers' bonds with their children. In these families, children are drawn into alliances with the father's family who may subject the mother to a range of controlling and denigrating behaviours.

Living in a setting where domestic violence is ongoing is likely to impact on mothers' capacity to manage both child care and household tasks. The survey of mothers in Sure Start programme areas in England undertaken in 2006 as part of the Sure Start impact study found that 'home chaos and mother's malaise' were strongly correlated with reports of domestic abuse (Ball and Niven 2007). Humphreys et al's (2009) exploratory UK study highlighted the sleep disruption experienced by mothers and children as a consequence of domestic violence and noted that mothers struggled to balance their own needs for sleep and their children's wakefulness. Mothers reported using prescribed medication and drugs to assist with their own sleep problems and this combination of self-medication and sleep disruption clearly has the potential to restrict parenting capacity. Mothering may also be circumscribed by the anticipation of violence and the need to placate their abusive partner so that children's needs have to take second place (see Humphreys et al 2006a).

However, mothers also describe making conscious efforts to protect their children and their parenting from the effects of domestic violence. Lapierre (2010) identifies a range of strategies and tactics adopted by mothers participating in his study which were aimed at managing their partner's violence and shielding the children:

> 'I just remember just trying to get the kids out of the way whenever he comes in. I would try and make sure that they were in bed.'

> (Shelly, quoted in Lapierre 2010, p350)

> 'You try your best so the kids can't hear. I was used to put the hi-fi on, the music up loud … Make sure that the doors are closed.'

> (Sunita, quoted in Lapierre 2010, p350)

These findings indicate that many mothers will have an awareness of the need to protect their children from exposure to domestic violence even if they struggle to achieve it.

Damant et al's (2010) qualitative study involved interviews with 27 mothers from Quebec, Canada, who had experienced domestic violence and whose children were known to have been abused. While their male partners had been primarily responsible for the abuse of the children, the women acknowledged their own capacity for losing control and engaging in abusive behaviour towards their children. This occurred in a context of heightened behaviour and fear and, in some cases, in response to abusive behaviour from children towards their mothers. A number of participants in this study reported that their parenting improved once their own experience of abuse ended:

> 'I would say that it was mainly when I was with my ex-partner that I was shouting ... But when he was gone, when I got him arrested, I was so stressed ... For a while I was shouting quite a lot, sometimes for no reason ... We were getting up in the morning and there was a storm in the house ... But it has been calmer for a while.'

> (Study participant, quoted in Damant et al 2010, p16)

Larger-scale North American studies have aimed to distinguish between different aspects of mothers' parenting and to look at changes in parenting skills over time. Levendosky and Graham-Bermann's (2000) research with 95 women and their children explored the impact of domestic violence on mothers' parenting. They found that although experience of domestic violence was associated with mothers' reduced warmth in parenting, it was not associated with more or less authoritative parenting. A subsequent study of 103 pre-school children and their mothers (Levendosky et al 2003) found that the women who were most severely abused reported more effective parenting and more secure attachments to their children. However, direct observation of mothers and their children found that children interacted less positively with mothers who had been victims of domestic abuse than with those who had not. Chapter 2 identified depression as a risk factor for the adverse effects of domestic violence on children and this study found that the psychological functioning of mothers was key in that those women who were found to be depressed or traumatised by their experience of domestic violence reported less effective parenting.

A national Canadian longitudinal study (Letourneau et al 2007), which surveyed mothers on their parenting at two-year intervals between 1994-95 and 2003-04, produced similar findings with regard to the capacity of mothers' parenting to recover from domestic violence. The researchers compared the parenting of 208 mothers whose children were exposed to domestic violence between the ages of 24 and 37 months with that of 3,037 mothers whose children were not. While those mothers whose children had been exposed to domestic violence initially reported lower levels of positive discipline, warm and nurturing behaviours and consistent parenting, they also showed a greater increase in positive discipline and less of a decrease in warm and nurturing behaviours over time compared to mothers not experiencing domestic violence. The researchers argue that mothers whose children were exposed to domestic violence may have sought to compensate for these experiences with increased levels of sensitivity and care. Maternal depression also played a crucial role in this study as it was found to reduce initial levels of positive discipline, while family dysfunction lowered all three types of parenting behaviour. Together, these studies suggest that the parenting of mothers experiencing domestic violence is not inevitably undermined, but that it is more likely to be so in the presence of maternal depression and other forms of adversity.

For those delivering children's services, Casanueva et al's (2008) US research is a relevant quantitative study examining mothers' parenting in a random sample of 1,943 families referred to child protective services. Mothers' parenting, mental health and experience of domestic violence were assessed using face-to-face interviews and a range of validated measures. The study found few significant statistical differences between the parenting of those mothers who had never experienced domestic violence, those who had experienced it in the past and those who were experiencing it in the present. For instance, there was no significant difference in the frequency with which spanking was used by these three groups of mothers. However, mothers who had experienced domestic violence in the past but were no longer doing so scored slightly higher on parenting measures than those who were currently exposed to domestic violence. This suggests, in common with Letourneau et al's (2007) study described above, that parenting can recover from the effects of domestic violence.

Kelleher et al's (2008b) research drew on data from the same national sample of families in contact with child protective services in the US, but where Casenueva et al (2008) used data on families with children under ten from the National Survey of Child and Adolescent Well-Being, Kelleher et al's sample included the mothers of one to fourteen-year-olds. Kelleher et al note that reports of aggressive and neglectful parenting behaviours were generally high in this sample of mothers in contact with child protective services, but they found that women who had experienced recent domestic violence (defined as physical violence in the last year) reported higher rates of physically aggressive and neglectful disciplinary behaviours. As a group, women who had experienced domestic violence, both in the past and recently, were found to report higher levels of aggressive and neglectful parenting behaviours than those who had not experienced domestic violence.

This last finding seems to contradict those of Casenueva et al (2008), despite the two samples being drawn from the same national database. This discrepancy may be accounted for by the inclusion in Kelleher et al's sample of older children who had been exposed to domestic violence for longer and were consequently more challenging. Or perhaps the different findings illustrate the lack of sensitivity of quantitative studies that rely on identifying statistical associations rather than exploring mothers and children's accounts of experience. Nevertheless, both studies provide evidence for the capacity of mothers' parenting to recover from the effects of domestic violence.

Parenting in the absence of community support

Parenting does not occur in a vacuum and untangling the effects of domestic violence from those of poverty, poor housing, low levels of physical and/or mental health can be challenging for research. The previous chapter identified social support as a factor that can enhance children's resilience, but domestic violence can act to cut women off from family and friends, either as a consequence of the isolating effects of the abuse itself or through leaving an abusive home. One British study of parenting (Ghate and Hazel 2004) found that parents with conflicted or unsupported relationships were among the groups most likely to describe restricted access to social support and/or a sense of being inadequately supported. Useful indicators of informal support utilised by this study that could be adapted for use in other contexts were: whether parents could usually leave their child for a day or overnight if necessary, whether they could get a lift to an important appointment and whether they could borrow more than £10.

Levendosky and Graham-Berrman (2001) found that low levels of social support together with adverse life events contributed to poorer psychological functioning of mothers experiencing domestic violence, which in turn undermined their parenting. Research with 145 African American women and their children who had used hospital services in a Southern US state found that those who had experienced domestic violence in the last year reported higher levels of parenting stress and less use of social support than those who had not experienced domestic violence (Mitchell et al 2006).

Participants in Lapierre's (2010) UK research commented on the lack of social support available once they had left abusive relationships:

> 'They re-house you and it's somewhere totally new: you don't know anybody, you don't know where the shops are, you don't know where the bus stop is, you don't know where the school is, you know nothing.'
>
> (Angela, quoted in Lapierre 2010, p347)

Isolation may be particularly acute for those survivors who are forced to sever their ties with close-knit minority ethnic communities through fear of being tracked down or subjected to reprisals. A UK study of minority women's experiences of leaving violent relationships (Burman and Chantler 2005) found that those who chose to be re-housed in predominantly white areas, in the hope of avoiding further contact with the perpetrator, could find themselves isolated and subject to racial abuse and violence. Similarly, mothers of children with disabilities may be particularly dependent on their partners for both financial and practical support. Their reliance on a network of local support services may make the prospect of leaving the family home particularly difficult, and they may risk being tracked down by the perpetrator if they seek to maintain those links (Baldry et al 2006).

Burman and Chantler (2004) noted that some BME women described being ejected from refuges and thrust into independence too early:

> 'You are going through suffering. I know they [refuge workers] are trying to put us on the right path by giving us our independence, pushing us to do things, so when I came here it was like get out of the door and do it for yourself and even though I can read and write English, I was scared. I didn't know which school the kids were going to, which post office to go to, they just told you, they just give you a map and go. And it's not easy.'
>
> (South Asian woman, quoted in Burman and Chantler 2004, p391)

Isolation also characterised the experiences of the disabled women included in Hague et al's (2008) study who described isolation both within abusive relationships and after leaving their partners. Homeless mothers also experience high levels of social isolation (Anooshian 2005), which reduces opportunities for their children to experience the supportive relationships with other adults that could contribute to resilience (see Chapter 3). Linking mothers and children into supportive social networks should, therefore, be a principal objective of intervention with these groups. Box 4.1 summarises key findings on the parenting of mothers experiencing domestic violence.

Box 4.1: Key findings on the parenting of mothers experiencing domestic violence

> Mothers' parenting may be undermined by assaults on self-esteem, by perpetrators forging hostile alliances with children or other family members, by the need to anticipate and avoid violence, and by sleep loss.

> Mental health needs and substance misuse resulting from the abuse can act to reduce parenting capacity in mothers.

> Mothers' ability to maintain positive discipline in the context of domestic violence is particularly likely to be affected.

> Mothers experiencing domestic violence are likely to have low levels of social support, both while they are in abusive relationships and after leaving. This will undermine their parenting capacity further.

> Mothers' parenting can recover from the effects of domestic violence.

Fathers' parenting

This review has already noted the neglect of fathers in research on domestic violence. While there is a substantial body of research on perpetrators, this rarely conceptualises them as fathers and various commentators (Guille 2004; Hester 2005; Featherstone and Peckover 2007) have highlighted this separation of fathers and perpetrators in both literature and practice and have argued for more research exploring the parenting of abusive men. While perpetrators are known to be a diverse group, Guille argues that some of their characteristics, such as histories of childhood abuse and high levels of substance abuse (see Chapter 2 of this review), together with the frequency of personality disorder in this population, are likely to impact on their parenting. Her review also indicates that men's understandings of their role as fathers, as well as their capacity to acknowledge and take responsibility for their abusive behaviour, may be key to the quality of their parenting.

In their Tennessee survey of 3,234 men convicted of a domestic violence offence who also had a fathering role, Salisbury et al (2009) found that while the majority agreed their children were exposed to interparental conflict, most did not consider that their children were affected by this experience. This reluctance to acknowledge the negative impact of exposure to domestic violence for children conveys both a resistance to assuming responsibility for harm and a need for information and education concerning the effects of domestic violence on children. Råkil's (2006) account of the work of the Norwegian Alternative to Violence service for abusive fathers demonstrates how this can be translated into practice. The first phase of work with men using this service involves a reconstruction of the violence, which includes detailed questions about the whereabouts of the children and their responses to what they saw/heard. This approach aims to change men's perceptions of their own violence, since behaviour that is not considered problematic is unlikely to change. Research on men's views of domestic violence (Stanley et al 2009) found that messages about the effects of domestic violence on children were rated as those most likely to prompt men to seek to change their behaviour:

> 'Well if he's likely to change, if he wants to change, he's going to change for his kids, isn't he?'
>
> (Father, quoted in Stanley et al 2009, p74)

A US study aimed to discriminate between the various types of relationship that are found between the abusive father figure and the child (Sullivan et al 2000). The researchers collected data from 80 mothers and their children (recruited from shelters and social services agencies) on the quality of children's relationships with different types of father figure. Those perpetrators who were the children's biological fathers were described as the most emotionally available to them; step-fathers were more abusive towards children than either biological fathers or non-father figures, and children reported being more fearful of them. However, Israel and Stover's (2009) study of 80 children aged 2 to 18 who had experienced domestic violence found that children's levels of adjustment were not explained by whether the perpetrator was their biological father or not, although children who had multiple father figures had significantly more negative behavioural symptoms than other children in the sample. A telephone survey of 107 women using domestic violence services in four US cities (Lee et al 2008) also provides a cautionary note. This study found no differences in the reported effects of domestic violence on children between those who were involved with child protective services and those who were not, but families where the perpetrator was the children's biological father were much less likely to have been referred to child protective services. The authors suggest that the perpetrator's status as biological father should not be a factor that influences referral to child protection services. Findings such as these should alert practitioners to the importance of recording the legal status of father figures in households with children. An audit of 67 social services case files in England (Featherstone 2009) discovered that the child's birth father was not identified in nearly a fifth of cases, and in a quarter of cases reviewed there was no information available on the parental responsibility of the father.

Research that explores the quality of abusive men's relationships with their children is gradually emerging. Bancroft and Silverman (2002) draw on their clinical experience of working with perpetrators and the earlier literature to paint a picture of abusive men as rigid and authoritarian in their parenting, under-involved and neglectful, while requiring that children meet their father's needs rather than vice versa. Data from a US national household survey has been used to distinguish between the fathering of violent men and non-violent men (Fox and Benson 2004). The analysis found that violent men used more punitive behaviours and fewer positive parenting behaviours than non-violent men, but as a group they did not differ from non-violent men in the amount of time they spent with children or in the way they monitored their children's behaviour.

Harne's (2004) research with 20 men on perpetrator programmes in England is one of the few UK studies to address the parenting of abusive men. She found that these men spent considerable amounts of time in sole charge of small children: two-thirds of her sample described themselves as regularly undertaking child care for children under the age of six for a few hours a day. Fathers' accounts included descriptions of being 'provoked' into abusive behaviour by children who failed to conform to the demands made of them:

'... They were terrified of me – all I had to do was look – I was quite cruel to be honest with you, for example at meal-times I used to sit there and make them eat things they really did not like and they used to cry. I wanted to make them too perfect – I wanted to make them what I should be like.'

(Father on a perpetrator programme, quoted in Harne 2004, p7)

Perel and Peled (2008) conducted in-depth interviews with 14 Israeli men known to have been violent to their partners in the last year who depicted their parenting as limited and constricted. They saw themselves as confined to an authoritarian role where their key identity was that of breadwinner and parenting was dominated by the mother. However, the men aspired to an image of 'good fatherhood' and expressed a desire for closer relationships with their children. The researchers suggest that this desire for a closer relationship with their children may be one factor fuelling men's battles for contact with their children and that such battles should not be interpreted purely as attempts to maintain control over their former partner. They characterise abusive fathers as 'simultaneously harmful and vulnerable' (Perel and Peled 2008) and suggest that intervention should alert them to the harm they are doing to their children and aim to end it, while acknowledging their distress and providing them with support.

Experiencing domestic violence in the context of contact

Chapter 2 noted that children frequently experience domestic violence in the setting of contact arrangements and some studies have explored children's experience and views of post-separation contact. Stover et al's (2003) research produces evidence for children's dual response to contact with abusive fathers. This Californian study collected data from 50 mothers and pre-school children who had been referred for child-parent psychotherapy following domestic violence but where the abuser was now living away from the family. The study examined the impact of contact visits on children's behaviour and found that those children who had weekly contact with their father showed fewer depressive, anxious and somatic symptoms. However, those children whose fathers had perpetrated more severe forms of violence had more symptoms of aggressive and antisocial behaviour, regardless of the frequency of contact. The research did not examine the quality of fathers' parenting during access, nor whether contact was a means of perpetuating abuse of children's mothers. The authors note that while their study offers evidence of children's attachment to abusive fathers, it also argues the need for determining access on a case-by-case basis.

Peled (2000) describes children as torn between conflicting responses to their fathers' violence: on the one hand, they may be attached to their father who may be perceived as the powerful person in the family; on the other, they fear and may condemn his violence. Her Israeli study (Peled 1998) of the views of 14 pre-adolescent children who had experienced domestic violence found that few managed to integrate these two opposing views; rather they embraced one or the other. Eriksson (2009) interviewed 17 Swedish children aged between 8 and 17 who described their experiences of being interviewed by social workers preparing reports for the family court in the light of the children's exposure to domestic violence. The children varied in whether or not they continued to see their fathers and whether they wanted to do so. However, few felt that social workers allowed them to participate in decisions being made about plans for future contact. In one case, a child's disclosure to the social worker that his father had hit him and that he was frightened of his father was fed back to his father via the report, resulting in further abuse.

Q:
You say that you trusted her [the investigator]; were you in any way afraid that mum or dad would find out what you had said?

Johan:
'I was scared that my dad would because, when he got to see the papers about what I had said, he got angry and hit me then too.'

(Eriksson 2009, p437)

An expert report produced for the Court of Appeal in England (Sturge and Glaser 2000) defined those situations where contact might be harmful. It argued that children who do not want contact should have their views heard and that decisions should be based on their views.

UK research provides evidence for the various ways in which contact can be the means by which abuse is perpetuated post-separation. A study of 53 women in England who had experienced domestic violence (Radford et al 1997) found that the majority reported their children having witnessed their fathers' violence during contact. Fathers interrogated children for information on their mothers' living arrangements and involved them in plans to kill their mothers. Likewise, Humphreys and Thiara's (2003) survey of women using domestic violence services in the UK found that only four of the 49 women who had contact arrangements in place did not experience post-separation violence. Contact arrangements were used by perpetrators to track their former partners down and children were charged with conveying abusive and threatening messages to their mothers.

The evaluation of Independent Domestic Violence Advisor (IDVA) services in England reported that there was conflict over contact in 41 per cent of cases where women had children (Howarth et al 2009). Likewise, Stanley et al's (2010b) research found that 36 of 196 incidents of domestic violence took place in the context of men seeking access to their children or the family home while 26 happened in the setting of contact or handovers. Young people and survivors participating in this study emphasised the need for high-quality supervised contact services; however, this is a scarce resource (Sturge and Glaser 2000; Harrison 2006).

Fathers participating in Harne's (2004) study of abusive fathers expressed a sense of entitlement to contact with their children and had high expectations that children would provide them with emotional support and love in the setting of contact. They indicated that they sometimes struggled to put children's interests before their own in this context and that contact was employed as a means of conveying insults and threats to their former partners.

Similarly, Johnston's (2006) US review of research and practice describes the separation anxiety some parents experience on divorce and notes that fear of abandonment can be projected onto children in the process of contact. Other studies that have collected women's and children's accounts of contact include examples of fathers threatening suicide and placing children on contact visits in situations where they are expected to prevent fathers harming themselves:

'I called ParentLine a lot because [my daughter] went off the rails a little bit. [My daughter] stayed with her dad on what she called his suicide watch, she was checking on him and he was coming into her bedroom at night waking her up and saying "I need to talk" and "I am so distraught about your mum and about what happened".'

(Christine, a survivor, quoted in Stanley et al 2010c, p40)

Johnston (2006) notes how, in the context of divorce and separation, acute feelings of pain and loss can be attributed to the 'bad' partner and these distortions can collide with and confuse accounts of domestic abuse. Family courts have been much criticised for a presumption of contact in relation to domestic violence (Radford and Hester 2006) and Johnston suggests that a hierarchy of guiding principles should inform such decisions. This hierarchy is also relevant for social workers intervening in families experiencing domestic violence who may occasionally question whether parents' accounts of abusive behaviour by their former partner reflect post-separation distress rather than fact. Johnston suggests the initial aim should be to achieve all five priorities listed in Box 4.2 but proposes that conflicts that occur in relation to the higher priorities are resolved by abandoning lower priorities.

Box 4.2: A hierarchy of priorities to inform decisions about child contact

Priority 1: Protect children directly from abusive and violent environments.

Priority 2: Support the safety and well-being of parents who are victims of abuse (with the assumption that they will then be better able to protect their child).

Priority 3: Respect the right of adult victims (empower them) to make their own decisions and direct their own lives.

Priority 4: Hold perpetrators accountable for their abusive behaviour (ie have them acknowledge their problem and take measures to correct it).

Priority 5: Allow children access to both parents.

(Johnston 2006, p29)

Chapter four: Summary

> Research includes accounts both of mothers' attempts to maintain positive parenting in the face of domestic violence and of mothers who acknowledge that domestic violence undermines their parenting.

> In the context of domestic violence, mothers' parenting may be undermined by assaults on their self-esteem and confidence, by perpetrators forging hostile alliances with children or other family members, by the need to anticipate and avoid violence, and by sleep loss, substance misuse and mental health needs.

> There is considerable evidence for the capacity of depression to affect the parenting of mothers experiencing domestic violence and so impact on children.

> While mothers' parenting appears to be adversely affected by domestic violence, there is evidence that their parenting can recover once they are no longer living with domestic violence.

> A lack of social support contributes to parenting problems and victims of domestic violence may have limited access to social support while they are in an abusive relationship and once they have left. This isolation may be particularly acute for BME mothers, mothers with disabilities, families with disabled children and homeless mothers and children. Interventions for these groups could be directed at linking them into relevant support systems.

> While research on the parenting of perpetrators is limited, there is some evidence that their parenting is more punitive. Identified perpetrator characteristics, such as substance misuse and mental health problems, are likely to interact with abusive and controlling patterns of behaviour to adversely affect parenting.

> Perpetrators frequently struggle to acknowledge the impact of their violence and abuse on children and this needs to be addressed in interventions for them – awareness of the effects of domestic violence on children can provide motivation for change.

> The evidence regarding differences in the parenting of biological and non-biological fathers is currently unclear. However, practitioners should ensure that they record information on the legal status of abusive fathers.

> Fathers' post-separation parenting may be distinguished by the continuation of abuse and manifestations of separation anxiety, which impact on children's well-being.

> Children are likely to vary in whether they wish to continue to see an abusive parent. Practitioners should give children the opportunity to participate freely in decisions about future contact with abusive fathers and respect their views on this question.

> In making decisions about contact, priority should be given to protecting children from exposure to violence and abusive behaviour.

Chapter five

Violence in Young People's Intimate Relationships

This chapter considers violence in young people's own intimate relationships. In particular, it looks at the evidence relating to:

> the prevalence of violence and abusive behaviour within young people's personal relationships, both within the general population and among specific and potentially vulnerable groups, including pregnant girls, young mothers, young offenders and looked after young people

> young people's attitudes towards abusive behaviour within relationships and their understanding of its nature and its impact

> the link between exposure to domestic violence in childhood and experience of violence in intimate relationships as a young person

> the effectiveness of programmes that aim to prevent violence in young people's relationships, including school-based PSHE programmes in the UK

> interventions that aim to help young people who are experiencing violence in their own relationships.

A summary of key findings is set out at the end of the chapter.

Chapter 3 of this review highlighted young people's peer relationships as a source of support. However, peer relationships can also be a place where violence and abuse is experienced in intimate relationships. Until recently, much of the evidence concerning violence and abuse in young people's relationships was derived from large-scale North American surveys. These have identified a correlation between exposure to domestic violence in their parents' relationships and abuse in young people's intimate relationships (Simonelli et al 2002; Whitfield et al 2003). Barter's (2009) research review found that childhood experiences of abuse and neglect act to increase young people's vulnerability to abuse in their own relationships. Other forms of violence in their peer groups can also function as risk factors for abuse in young people's intimate relationships (Schnurr and Lohmann 2008; Barter 2009). Violence in young people's intimate relationships has been linked to mental health problems, depression and suicide (Silverman et al 2001; Collin-Vézina et al 2006), as well as to the experience of domestic violence in adult relationships (O'Leary et al 1989; Cleveland et al 2003).

Violence in young people's relationships – a UK study

Barter et al's (2009) study illuminates the UK picture. This research utilised a survey of 1,353 young people aged between 13 and 16 in eight schools in England, Scotland and Wales and 91 interviews that explored young people's experiences of interpersonal violence in their own and their friends' relationships. Key findings are summarised in Box 5.1 (overleaf).

> **Box 5.1: Partner exploitation and violence in teenage intimate relationships in the UK**
>
> > Three-quarters of girls in a relationship experienced emotional violence, a third reported sexual violence and a quarter had experienced physical violence.
>
> > When all forms of violence were considered together, one in six girls reported severe levels of violence.
>
> > Half of those boys in a relationship experienced emotional violence, 18 per cent experienced physical violence and 16 per cent sexual violence.
>
> > While the majority of girls reported that the violence they experienced had a negative effect on their well-being, only a minority of boys did so.
>
> > Sexual violence was particularly likely to have an adverse impact on girls.
>
> > Mobile telephones and social networking sites were also means by which girls were subjected to coercion and control.
>
> (Barter et al 2009)

The authors conclude that boys are less aware than girls of the harmful impact of abusive behaviour and that prevention and intervention programmes for young people need to address this issue.

A NSPCC prevalence study (Radford et al forthcoming 2011) found lower lifetime rates of intimate partner victimisation than Barter et al (2009), with 7.9 per cent of 11 to 17-year-olds and 12.7 per cent of 18 to 24-year-olds reporting abuse from an intimate partner. These lower figures are attributable to the inclusion in the NSPCC study of younger children who had not necessarily experienced an intimate partner relationship in their lifetime. Five per cent of 11 to 17-year-olds surveyed in the NSPCC study reported experiencing some form of victimisation from an intimate partner in the last 12 months. In common with Barter et al's (2009) research, the NSPCC study found that girls reported much higher impact of partner violence with 47.3 per cent of girls reporting being hurt or injured, compared with 20.8 per cent of boys. Moreover, exposure to sexual or physical assault was significantly associated with raised levels of trauma-related symptoms among girls, but not among boys. Physical assault by a same-sex partner was also associated with poorer emotional well-being in both boys and girls, suggesting that this issue also needs to be acknowledged and built into prevention and intervention strategies.

Various studies have explored the attitudes and knowledge that inform young people's abusive behaviour. While some research with young people in the UK (Mullender et al 2002; Bell and Stanley 2006) found them to be confused about what domestic violence was, McCarry's (2009) study in Scotland found that young people had absorbed recent campaign messages about the nature of domestic violence. However, the young people participating in her school focus groups were resistant to the view that men are the primary perpetrators of domestic abuse and found justifications for male violence. McCarry argues that these young people continued to subscribe to a traditional patriarchal model of gender relations that legitimated men's use of violence.

Violence in the intimate relationships
of vulnerable young people

The association noted between childhood experience of abuse and/or neglect and abuse in young people's intimate relationships makes it particularly likely that young people in contact with children's services will experience such problems. Two Canadian studies have explored the relationships of young people involved with child protection services. Collin-Vézina et al (2006) examined experiences of relationship violence among 220 adolescent girls living in out-of-home care. The majority of the sample reported experiencing some form of dating violence, with 28 per cent reporting severe victimisation but no major injury, and 25 per cent reporting severe injuries. The more severely injured group reported more negative self-concepts than girls who described low levels of or no dating violence.

A Canadian study (Wekerle et al 2009) of 402 adolescents drawn from child protection workers' caseloads found that most of the girls and nearly half the boys reported some degree of dating violence. Behaviour that involved physical assault was experienced by 13 to 21 per cent of the sample – substantially higher than the 10 per cent national average. The study found that experience of emotional abuse predicted all forms of dating violence in boys and dating victimisation in girls. This study employed a broad definition of emotional abuse (parents saying hurtful things), which was also found to predict PTSD symptoms. The authors argue that PTSD acts as a mediator between emotional abuse and dating violence. They suggest that as young people rarely disclose such information spontaneously, social workers need to increase their alertness to the possibility of young people experiencing violence and abuse in their intimate relationships and to implement routine questioning about this issue.

In the UK, Wood et al (forthcoming 2011) built on Barter et al's (2009) study of the general population with research that focused on disadvantaged young people. Interviews with 82 young people drawn from a range of settings (such as a project for young people excluded from school, a project for young mothers, a young offenders' institution, children's homes and a special school) found that over half the girls reported having been a victim of physical violence in at least one of their relationships. This figure contrasts with just under a quarter of the girls participating in Barter et al's (2009) general population survey. A quarter of the girls in Wood et al's (forthcoming 2011) study reported more severe forms of violence, as compared with 11 per cent of girls in the general population study. Many of the disadvantaged girls participating in Wood et al's research normalised the violence they experienced and minimised its seriousness, although they reported that it impacted on their welfare; half the girls in this study saw partner control as an integral aspect of relationships and as proof of intimacy. Boys in this study were less likely to differ in their experiences of violence in relationships from those in the general population study, and they were less likely than the girls to say that they were affected by violence.

The majority of the 16 pregnant girls and young mothers interviewed by Wood et al (forthcoming 2011) reported experiencing physical violence in their relationships and this was consistent with findings from other studies examining the relationship between young pregnancy and domestic violence. Sexual pressure and force were also issues for this group of young women, who reported that their partner's controlling behaviour often increased following the birth. Young women in this group were aware of the harmful effects on their children of exposure to domestic violence and some cited this as a reason for ending the relationship. Others were dependent on abusive partners for financial and emotional support and were anxious to avoid the stigma attached to being a young single parent. These young women were wary of children's services as they feared losing their children. They also perceived the demands of social workers to be unrealistic and were themselves in need of safeguarding.

> Michelle:
> ... They say you do this, you do this, for your daughter, but they don't turn around and think like I'm sat there with a black eye, battered, and they're telling me I've got to do this, do this, when I haven't even got the strength to think straight, let alone, take action against him ... they're saying get certain things against him and I'm saying that won't phase him, he's not scared.

> Interviewer:
> ... How did that make you feel?

> Michelle:
> Bad, I felt that I was being victimised, I was already a victim and I was being victimised by social services ... 'Cos they were saying you have to do this, your child is gonna be out on the at risk register ... it seemed to me that I was the one getting abused but I was getting all the blame, they didn't do nothing towards him.

> (Wood et al forthcoming 2011)

Looked after young women participating in this study were especially vulnerable to sexual violence, often from older men. Many of them had been exposed to domestic violence in their parents' relationships. They reported that foster carers and residential workers failed to take their relationship difficulties seriously.

An association between isolation and domestic violence has been noted in previous chapters of this review and care leavers living alone appeared to be at high risk of partner violence. The authors recommend that specific programmes be developed and delivered to prepare looked after children and care leavers for dealing with violence and control in intimate relationships.

Prevention programmes for children and young people

Programmes aimed at preventing violence in young people's intimate relationships have been delivered in North America since the mid-1980s (Jaffe et al 1992; Avery-Leaf et al 1997; Foshee et al 1998; Wolfe and Jaffe 1999). From the mid-1990s onwards, similar programmes began to emerge in the UK (Stanley et al 2010a). Ellis's (2004) mapping study in England, Wales and Northern Ireland identified 102 local authorities where such programmes had been delivered; 82 per cent of these programmes addressed domestic violence and 40 per cent 'dating' violence.

While Ellis (2004) found such programmes were often initiated by specialist domestic violence organisations or crime partnerships, the majority of programmes identified by her mapping study were delivered in mainstream schools, with just over a third also running in special schools. Increasingly, programmes are located in the PSHE (Personal, Social and Health Education) curriculum. However, Ellis (2008) notes that school staff may feel ill-equipped to deliver such programmes, particularly with regard to managing disclosures. While practitioners from specialist domestic violence agencies may provide relevant expertise, such input is difficult to sustain over time and reliance on external agencies to deliver programmes in schools may result in one-off initiatives that are not reinforced or sustained (Bell and Stanley 2006; Stanley et al 2010a).

Programmes usually embrace a range of goals, which include raising children and young people's awareness of domestic violence, offering support to those living with domestic violence and identifying and promoting positive behaviour in young people's relationships. Ellis's (2004) survey found that schools targeted programmes at under-16s, with 34 per cent of programmes aimed at both primary and secondary school pupils, 11 per cent targeted the 5 to 11 age group and 54 per cent were directed at secondary school students. Most programmes are delivered to a mixed-gender audience, although 41 per cent of the programmes surveyed by Ellis included some single-sex components (Ellis 2004). A number of established models (London Borough of Islington 1994; Sandwell Against Domestic Violence 2000; Debbonaire and Westminster Domestic Violence Forum 2002; Protective Behaviours UK 2004) have influenced the design and content of programmes in the UK. These utilise a range of group activities and techniques; participative and action-oriented learning approaches, such as the use of role-play and theatre, have been shown to be particularly appreciated by boys (Bell and Stanley 2006). However, the extent to which programmes focus on gender equality varies according to the model employed and the attitudes and perspectives of those delivering the programmes (Hester and Westmarland 2005; Stanley et al 2010a).

The length, frequency and number of sessions delivered have been found to vary considerably with little apparent rationale for these differences in length and intensity (Ellis 2008; Whitaker et al 2006). Bell and Stanley's (2006) evaluation of a Healthy Relationships Programme in northern England found that some of the attitudinal changes achieved immediately following the programme were not sustained at follow-up, which suggests that programmes need to be reinforced by repetition during children's school careers.

> 'I would like to have it again in year 11 so I could keep it in mind – to learn it again in case I forgot.'
>
> (Boy participating in the Healthy Relationships Programme, quoted in Stanley et al 2010a)

Evaluations of programmes conducted in the UK (Reid Howie Associates 2001; Hester and Westmarland 2005; Bell and Stanley 2006) indicate they have had success in increasing children and young people's awareness and understanding of domestic violence and their knowledge about relevant sources of help, as well as achieving some attitudinal changes (Ellis 2008). However, to date, there is little UK evidence available concerning the capacity of these programmes to achieve behavioural change or to sustain change over time.

Larger-scale evaluations of programme impact have been undertaken in the US. Wekerle and Wolfe (1999) reported on the evaluations from six dating-violence prevention programmes and found that the programmes achieved a reduction in negative attitudes towards violence in young people's relationships as well as an increased knowledge and understanding about domestic violence. Foshee et al (1996; 2000; 2004) conducted a randomised-controlled trial of the Safe Dates programme, which was delivered to 1,603 eighth and ninth-grade pupils in 14 public schools in North Carolina. The treatment group received a theatre production and ten 45-minute taught sessions. Compared with the control group, pupils receiving the programme experienced between 56 and 92 per cent less violence victimisation and perpetration of moderate dating violence; however, these effects were not identified for severe physical violence. Positive changes in attitudes towards gender stereotyping, conflict resolution skills and awareness of community services were also reported. Some of the positive behaviour changes noted following the programme were not in evidence one year after the programme, although factors found to mediate dating violence such as conflict management and awareness of dating violence services were maintained (Foshee et al, 2004). Box 5.2 summarises the available evidence on preventive programmes for children and young people.

> **Box 5.2: Preventive domestic violence programmes for children and young people**
>
> > Preventive programmes are delivered to both primary and secondary pupils in the context of personal, social, health and economic education (PSHE).
>
> > It is unclear what length, intensity and frequency of programme delivery are most effective.
>
> > Programmes have been successful in increasing awareness and understanding of domestic violence and informing participants about sources of help.
>
> > Some of these changes may not be sustained without further input.
>
> > The evidence for programmes achieving sustained behavioural change is as yet limited.

Support for and interventions with young people experiencing violence in their intimate relationships

There is limited evidence available on interventions for either young people experiencing abuse in intimate relationships or for young perpetrators of abuse (Radford et al forthcoming 2011). Barter et al (2009) found that friends were the most likely source of support for young people experiencing violence in their relationships. However, advice from peers did not always appear to be beneficial, with some friends reinforcing expectations of abusive or submissive behaviours. The young people interviewed had only rarely disclosed their experience to professionals: school learning mentors were the group most likely to be the recipients of such disclosures. Young people valued the regular contact with mentors, which allowed for the development of a trusting relationship within which disclosure could take place. They also perceived the mentor's position outside the teaching structure to be helpful. Where mentors were recruited from the local Asian community, they were often perceived by Asian young people as having an enhanced understanding of young people's problems and they could act as a bridge between a young person and her family (Barter et al 2009).

The value of mentoring relationships for addressing problems in young people's intimate relationships is also highlighted by Banister and Leadbeater (2007), who describe an Australian group-mentoring programme. This intervention offered girls the opportunity to discuss dating violence, sexual health and relationship problems and assisted them in distinguishing abusive relationships. Banister and Leadbeater note that this form of support may be particularly valuable for girls who are alienated from their families and isolated by the abuse.

A study of 98 young people using a young people's mental health service in Melbourne, Australia (Brown et al 2009), found an association between experience of interpersonal violence and substance dependence that has been noted by other studies (Silverman et al 2001), as well as reduced levels of psychosocial functioning among young people experiencing interpersonal violence. Although the study did not examine the impact of mental health service provision for this group, the authors highlight the slightly higher proportion of young people experiencing violence in their intimate relationships in their sample than that found in general population surveys. They suggest that young people's mental health services should ask service users about violence in their intimate relationships and offer interventions designed to increase personal safety for victims and reduce abusive behaviour for perpetrators.

Young people participating in Barter et al's (2009) general population study rarely reported discussing violence in their own relationships with other professionals, including social workers, and there is little evidence available on the extent to which social workers address this issue in their work with young people. Among the disadvantaged young people participating in Wood et al's (forthcoming 2011) research, help-seeking was restricted by young people's fear that they would not be taken seriously by professionals, nor be believed. They were concerned that social workers would not respect their confidentiality or provide consistency of support. Social workers were also seen as focused on the whole family rather than on the young person. However, a minority of research participants described positive experiences of social workers having helped them to discuss and manage their intimate relationships.

> Interviewer:
> So was it helpful talking to your social worker?
>
> Nikki:
> Yeah it was, she obviously chatted to loads of people in the same situation before, and she told me basically like, what to do and how to cope with things. And I just took to her really well, and, like I just got on with her. And it was ever since chatting to my social worker, that's when I like opened up and told everyone my problems instead of keeping it all in. I like lets people know what I'm thinking and stuff ... she did change my life really. If I wouldn't have had a social worker I probably would have been the same now, so it's good really.
>
> (Wood et al forthcoming 2011)

Since young people rarely report violence in their intimate relationships to professionals, the researchers recommend that social workers should routinely include questions about partner violence and control in their assessment of young people. This study also suggests that a switch in the focus of assessment away from the family to consider young people in the context of their peer and intimate relationships is required if young people's experiences of violence in their intimate relationships are to be addressed.

Chapter five: Summary

> Girls are more likely than boys to experience emotional, physical and sexual abuse in relationships; girls report adverse effects of abuse more often than boys, particularly from sexual abuse. Boys' awareness of the harmful effects of violence and abuse needs to be increased.

> Looked after young people, care leavers and young people in contact with the child protection system appear more likely than those in the general population to have experienced severe forms of violence and abuse in their relationships. Looked after young women appear especially vulnerable to sexual abuse from older men.

> Young mothers report high levels of abuse and violence in their relationships but are anxious about losing care of their children if they disclose this.

> Schools in the UK now deliver preventive programmes aimed at a range of age groups characterised by considerable variation in their length, content and frequency. While evaluations indicate the success of such programmes in raising young people's awareness of domestic violence and changing attitudes, there is as yet no evidence of behaviour change that is sustained over time.

> Friends are the likeliest source of support for young people experiencing abuse in their own relationships but advice from friends is not always beneficial.

> Young people have identified school-based mentors as a group they are likely to look to for support with abusive relationships. The intermediate, non-professional role of mentors may be helpful in this respect. Group mentoring has also been successfully used in this context.

> Young people do not see social workers as offering a confidential and consistent source of support and see them as family-focused rather than focused on the young person.

> All practitioners working with young people should consider routinely asking about violence and abuse in their intimate relationships since they are unlikely to disclose this issue spontaneously.

Chapter six

The Service Response – Screening, Assessment and Engagement

This chapter discusses the evidence for:

> the value of screening for domestic violence, including which factors are most likely to promote disclosure and in which settings

> how effective practitioners are in engaging children and young people in discussion about domestic violence, and what strategies are most likely to encourage children and young people to talk

> how effectively children's services respond to police notifications of domestic violence

> the effectiveness of the Common Assessment Framework and other assessment procedures in securing the appropriate support for families experiencing domestic violence, including the implications of a 'stop-start' approach characterised by a repeated pattern of assessment and short-term interventions

> children's services' interventions with violent fathers.

A summary of key findings is set out at the end of the chapter.

The evidence reviewed in previous chapters has shown that while children's exposure to domestic violence is widespread, not all children and young people will experience harm as a consequence. A key task is therefore to develop systems that will distinguish between those families that require intervention from children's services and those that require either other forms of intervention or support, or no services at all. Another recurrent theme in this review has been families' reluctance to disclose domestic violence to social care practitioners. This chapter therefore examines approaches that assist in the identification of families experiencing domestic violence and which promote engagement with services as well as considering what barriers exist to positive relationships with families. There is also an accumulating body of evidence that has examined social care interventions with families experiencing domestic violence and some consistent messages are emerging from both US and UK studies.

Identifying and screening for domestic violence in families

This review began by noting that a number of factors combine to make children and parents reluctant to disclose domestic violence to professionals, particularly social workers. Children and young people are most likely to seek help for domestic violence from friends, friends' parents and other family members (McGee 2000; Mullender et al 2002; Gorin 2004). Concerns about confidentiality may prevent them from approaching teachers or other authority figures (Buckley et al 2006). Various studies (see Stanley 1997) provide evidence for the ways in which fears of having children removed from their care act to restrict mothers' willingness to seek help for domestic violence from social services. 'The Day to Count' study (Stanko 2001) compared reports of domestic violence received by the police on a single day with the population of refuges in the UK and found that refuges housed more than twice the number of women who contacted police. This gives an indication of the extent to which incidents attended by the police and subsequently notified to children's services represent the 'tip of the iceberg'. Among men, masculine stereotypes can inhibit help-seeking (White and Johnson 2000; O'Brien et al 2005; White et al 2006) and male perpetrators of domestic violence often require some external stimulus to prompt them to seek help to change their behaviour (Hester et al 2006); Chapter 7 notes that this is often provided by children's services' interventions in families. Stanley et al's (2009) study of men's views and experiences of domestic violence found that the anonymity and confidentiality offered by telephone helplines made them men's preferred source of support concerning abusive behaviour, with GPs the second most frequently cited source of help.

Children's services' capacity to identify domestic violence as an issue in children's lives is therefore often dependent on information from other agencies and on the skills and tools used by the practitioner. In the 1980s and 1990s, children's social workers in England and Wales were much criticised for their failures to recognise the presence and impact of domestic violence in families (Maynard 1985; Farmer and Owen 1995; Stanley 1997). However, the inclusion of children's exposure to domestic violence in the Adoption and Children Act 2002 and police notifications of domestic violence incidents to children's services have served to alert social workers to the widespread presence of domestic violence in families referred to them. An analysis of social work interventions in cases notified to children's services by the police (Stanley et al 2010c) reported that social workers showed awareness of domestic violence and its impact on children in the families they worked with. A Northern Ireland study of child protection interventions with families experiencing domestic violence (Devaney 2008) also found that social workers evinced an awareness of domestic violence.

Where practitioner awareness of domestic violence in families remains low, screening tools may both raise detection rates and increase practitioners' sensitivity to the issue. To date, screening tools or routine enquiry have been primarily used with women rather than with children and young people or men. Magen et al (2000) developed a screening questionnaire for mothers to be used by child welfare preventive services in New York. They found that use of the questionnaire, together with the training that accompanied its implementation, resulted in a three-fold increase in the numbers of women identified as experiencing domestic violence. Women using the services appreciated being offered the opportunity to describe their experiences of domestic violence. In the UK, Hester (2006) described an initiative aimed at enabling NSPCC practitioners, health visitors and social care staff to use routine enquiry about domestic violence with mothers. In addition to incorporating routine enquiry into existing practice and protocols, staff were provided with training and opportunities to reflect on their experiences of adopting this new approach. In common with Magen et al's findings, identification of domestic violence by both health visitors and social care workers more than trebled over two years. Similarly, Bacchus et al (2004) found that identification rates increased substantially when routine enquiry about domestic violence was introduced by midwives in maternity clinics at a London hospital. The researchers concluded that women are unlikely to disclose experience of domestic violence unless asked directly.

Increasing practitioners' awareness of domestic violence through training appears to assist the implementation of routine enquiry. An overview of projects funded under the Home Office Crime Reduction programme (Hester and Westmarland 2005) found that where routine enquiry was introduced, it was most effective when incorporated into existing patterns of work. However, the aims of routine enquiry should extend beyond detection to the provision of services; ultimately, these should aim to end women and children's exposure to domestic violence (Wathen and MacMillan 2003). Routine enquiry therefore needs to be supported by relevant local services for those who disclose domestic violence and by established and clearly identified interagency pathways for practitioners to refer women and children to those services.

The Identification and Referral to Improve Safety (IRIS) project in London and Bristol is trialling a new approach aimed at increasing GPs' identification and management of women experiencing domestic violence (Gregory et al 2010). The intervention consists of two 2-hour training sessions delivered jointly by clinicians and domestic violence advocates, as well as a separate training session for administrative staff. It also includes: an electronic pop-up reminder in automated patients' records, which appears when particular symptoms associated with domestic violence are entered; an explicit referral pathway to a named advocate in local domestic violence projects; publicity materials on domestic violence; and 'project champions' in GP practices (Gregory et al 2010). Although results from the randomised controlled trial are not yet available, early findings indicate that a simple referral form that includes provision for GPs to receive feedback from domestic violence advocates has encouraged the identification and referral of victims (Johnson 2010). The fact that training was delivered by the same professionals who would receive and respond to referrals was also reported to be reassuring by GPs (Johnson 2010).

The most impressive evidence for the effectiveness of screening for domestic violence comes from a US study of screening in primary care and women and children's clinics. McFarlane et al (2005) screened mothers attending these clinics using two simple questions administered by nurses. They randomly assigned 360 women with experience of domestic violence in the last 12 months to either screening with a referral card only or to a nurse case-management service, which included supported care and advice together with a pre-designed safety brochure and support with referrals to relevant agencies. Standardised measures were used to collect parental reports of children's behaviours at the time of screening and 24 months later (233 mothers participated in follow-up). While most children's behaviour problems significantly improved over the 24 months, with scores for young children improving most, there were no significant differences found between the screening-only group and the mothers receiving nurse case management. The researchers suggest that disclosure in itself serves to break down the secrecy that perpetuates domestic violence and so reduces the experience of violence and its impact on children's behaviour.

Hester et al's (2007) overview advocates avoiding initial or screening interviews with women and children in the presence of their partners, as this is likely to impede disclosure of domestic violence. This makes settings such as the antenatal clinic or GP's surgery particularly appropriate for undertaking screening. However, women for whom English is not their first language may be more likely to attend these services with their partners; Lazenbatt and Greer (2009) note that partners' reluctance to leave women alone with the midwife is a major barrier to introducing screening in the antenatal clinic. Hester et al (2007) point out that women may feel unable to disclose abusive experiences immediately and that screening questions may need to be asked more than once. Box 6.1 lists questions that can be utilised for screening purposes.

Box 6.1: Screening questions to encourage disclosure of domestic violence

> How are things at home?

> How are arguments settled?

> How are decisions reached?

> What happens when you argue/disagree?

> Do you feel/have you ever felt frightened of your partner?

> Do you feel/have you ever felt threatened/intimidated by your partner?

> What happens when your partner gets angry?

> Does your partner shout at you, call you names, put you down?

> Has your partner ever physically hurt you? How? What happened?

> Has your partner ever thrown things?

> Has your partner ever destroyed things you care about?

> Has your partner ever forced you to have sex or engage in any sexual activities against your will?

> What do the children do when (any of the above) is happening?

> How do the children feel when (any of the above) is happening?

(Hester et al 2007, p180-181)

Talking to children about domestic violence

McGee's (2000) and Mullender et al's (2002) research with children experiencing domestic violence found that children and young people wanted opportunities to talk about domestic violence and wanted their accounts to be taken seriously. A survey of secondary-school children (Mullender et al 2002) reported that the opportunity to talk, together with reassurance and support, emerged as the most valuable form of help. Similarly, Stanley et al (2010c) found that young people valued police officers and social workers who listened to them, were accessible and provided them with information.

'I have, I tell you, one social worker I've got to give it and I want her mentioning, [social worker's name], oh she was just the best, 24 hours a day she would just be there, you know even if it was two o'clock at night, she'd be there, no problem, you know what I mean.'

(Ann, young people's focus group member, quoted in Stanley et al 2010c, p61)

Professionals who ignored or excluded children from their interactions with adults were seen as unhelpful:

'They listen to the adults more ... they don't want to talk to you.'

(Nicola, young people's focus group member, quoted in Stanley et al 2010c, p54)

Mullender et al (2002) also found that children were active in employing a range of coping strategies in response to their experiences of domestic violence and that they wanted this active role acknowledged by professionals. However, research continues to show that practitioners can be reluctant to talk directly to children about their experiences of domestic violence and to acknowledge their role as active participants both in the abuse and in decisions about future plans and interventions. A study of families' experiences of contact (Hester and Radford 1996) identified only eight out of 53 cases where court welfare officers asked children directly for their views about maintaining contact with the abusive parent. Doctorate research examining 70 Cafcass reports (Macdonald 2010) found that children's views were elicited by Cafcass staff, but often not in relation to their experience of domestic violence.

Eriksson (2009) analysed interviews with 17 children in Sweden aged 8 to 17 about their experience of social work intervention following their exposure to domestic violence. The social workers concerned were the equivalent of Cafcass officers, appointed to carry out an investigation and produce a report for the family law court. The analysis found that social workers varied in their capacity to talk directly with the child about their experiences of violence and to acknowledge their identity as a victim of domestic violence. They also differed in the extent to which they were prepared to provide children with the information and feedback they needed to participate in decisions about contact. Eriksson suggests that boys are less likely than girls to be recognised as victims by social workers, and are more likely to have their wishes not to have contact with abusive fathers ignored. She advocates reflexivity to ensure that social workers are not influenced by established notions of 'ideal victims' in their communication. She also argues that children experiencing domestic violence need to be approached both as victims and as actors with the capacity to contribute to plans and decisions.

Faller (2003) focuses on communicating with children about domestic violence at the micro-level and identifies three different approaches to talking to children about their experiences of domestic violence. These are shown in Box 6.2.

Box 6.2: Talking to children about domestic violence

1: **Cognitive interviewing** – an approach, developed from criminal investigations, which involves reconstruction of the context of a domestic violence incident. The child is asked to: 'Make a picture in your head' or to draw a particular scene or event. They are then asked to describe everything they can remember, from the beginning to the middle to the end, not leaving anything out.

2: **Narrative elaboration** – this approach is suitable for children aged 6 to 11 and involves the use of cue cards showing pictures of scenes representing family members, actions, emotions and resolutions of events. These cards are used to trigger discussion. Children need to be rehearsed in their use.

3: **Segmentation** – once a child has exhausted their initial recollection of an incident they can be asked to tell everything they remember about what happened in segments – for example: 'What happened after your mum went into the living room?'

(Faller 2003)

Faller also identifies a range of open-ended and invitational questions that can be used to explore the impact of domestic violence with children. She recommends that children be asked about their sleep patterns, emotions and behaviours and suggests the following questions:

> How do you sleep?

> Do you ever have nightmares?

> Tell me about your nightmares.

> What is the scariest thing that has ever happened to you?

> Do you ever get so angry that you want to hurt someone?

> Tell me about what you do.

(Faller 2003, p383)

Children and young people need to talk about domestic violence and have their experiences acknowledged and validated, and they need to be able to do this in a confidential and discrete setting. Focus-group research with children and young people in Ireland (Buckley et al 2007) reported that embarrassment and fears of being bullied by peers were identified as barriers to talking about domestic violence in school or with friends. A study involving 19 young people in rural England found that these concerns can be magnified in rural areas, where young people experience high visibility (Stalford et al 2003). Barter et al (2009) emphasise young people's needs for confidentiality in relation to disclosing violence in their own intimate relationships. Similar fears have been identified among young people in relation to discussion of other sensitive and stigmatised topics such as sexual health. A useful strategy adopted in relation to sexual health services in such communities and in schools is to offer them under the umbrella of other less stigmatised forms of support (Craig and Stanley 2006).

Children's services response to police notifications of families experiencing domestic violence

In England and Wales, police notifications of domestic violence incidents are the principal means by which children's services are informed about children's exposure to domestic violence. A range of commentators (Cleaver et al 2004; Social Services Inspectorate of Wales 2004; Rivett and Kelly 2006; Ofsted 2008) have noted the high volume of police notifications and the pressure this has created for children's services in the UK. Lord Laming's (2009) review of safeguarding services following the death of Baby Peter in Haringey recommended the establishment of the National Safeguarding Delivery Unit, which would 'urgently develop guidance on referral and assessment systems for children affected by domestic violence' (p87).

Similar problems in relation to referrals of domestic violence incidents are evident in Australia and North America where the volume of notifications may be augmented by the requirement for mandatory reporting. Humphreys (2008) argues that a statutory child protection response to notifications of incidents of domestic violence is 'not effective, efficacious, efficient or ethical' (p237) and suggests that resources for responding to the needs of children exposed to domestic violence should be diverted to the community sector. A critique of North American policy (Jaffe et al 2003) found that although classifying exposure to domestic violence as grounds for state intervention had led to an improvement in interagency collaboration, it also acted to overload child protection services and functioned as a deterrent to disclosure of domestic violence. Edleson (2004) proposes that children's experience of domestic violence should not automatically be defined as maltreatment and argues for the development of criteria or screening tools that would indicate the need for statutory intervention.

Recent research has provided an account of the ways in which children's services in England and Wales are managing police notifications. An evaluation of local authorities' implementation of the Assessment Framework found that police notifications featured among those referrals least likely to progress to an initial assessment (Cleaver and Walker 2004). A study of police notifications in two local authorities in England (Stanley et al 2010b) found that only 28 (15%) of the 184 families notified to children's services received an assessment or additional service; moreover, 19 of these were already open cases, which means that the notification system triggered a new service for just five per cent of families. Figure 6.1 shows that 60 per cent of families received a 'no further action' response from children's services. Three-quarters of these 'no further action' cases had no or low previous levels of involvement with children's social services in that authority (ie previous notifications or referrals that had been closed on receipt with no further action). The notification system therefore operated to draw large numbers of families into the child protection system only to release them without offering them a service. Social work managers participating in this study commented on the resources devoted to the task of filtering out notifications:

> 'I think we spend a lot of time trying to assess whether or not we should be involved ... that is very resource intensive regarding the actual resources I have to provide a front line service.'
>
> (Senior manager quoted in Stanley et al 2010b)

Figure 6.1: Social services' response to notified families

A
No Further Action
60%

B
Letters/Phone calls/Visits
25%

C
Safeguarding Service
10%

D
Family Support Service
5%

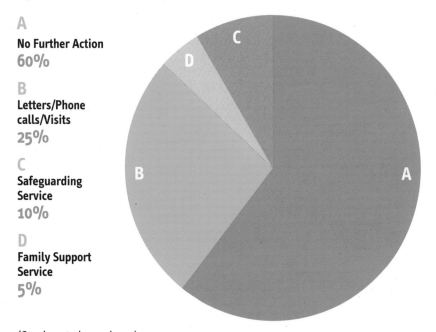

(Stanley et al 2010d, p10)

The finding that only a very small proportion of these children and families receive intervention from children's services raises two questions:

> What are the mechanisms for identifying those children and families where the risk is greatest?

> What early interventions are effective in meeting the needs of those children and families who do not meet the threshold for children's services' intervention?

Chapter 7 considers the research evidence on early intervention with children and families experiencing domestic violence. Stanley et al's (2010d) study identified a number of emerging interagency approaches to filtering notifications that aim to distinguish those children who require a Section 17 or Section 47 intervention. These approaches are discussed in Chapter 8, which addresses interagency work.

Communication with families

Letters

In one of the sites participating in Stanley et al's (2010b) study of children's services' responses to notifications of domestic violence incidents, letters were sent to families in the absence of any additional intervention. In most cases, these were families whose previous involvement with children's services was limited and where concerns were perceived to be low. Letters were commonly addressed to both parents where they were thought to be living together, although in one district letters were usually addressed to the mother. Researchers (Humphreys et al 2001; Stanley and Humphreys 2006) have drawn attention to the potential impact of such letters on family dynamics and the review (HMICA 2005) of Cafcass's performance in relation to domestic violence instructed one Cafcass district to cease sending out letters to both parents on safety grounds.

Some social workers participating in Stanley et al's (2010b) study were aware of the risks of sending such letters and described contacting victims by other methods, but they commented that notifications rarely provided them with victims' telephone numbers. Such letters can convey unfeasible expectations and, if addressed to the mother, can act to allocate responsibility for controlling her partner's abusive behaviour to the victim (Farmer 2006; Hester et al 2007). Practitioners were aware of how these letters might be received:

> 'I've had a phone call in the past where the woman I had written to was quite ... frustrated with the letter ... Because clearly she ... had tried very hard to keep her child safe and felt that it was the husband or the ex-partner's behaviour, that he should be the one that we should be addressing.'

> (Initial assessment worker, quoted in Stanley et al 2010b)

In the two sites participating in Stanley et al's study, practitioners drew on templates designed for cases that evoked low or high levels of concern to send letters to families. These often contained language that was both intimidating and impenetrable, as the two examples in Box 6.3 illustrate.

Box 6.3: Examples of letters sent to families experiencing domestic violence in the absence of other interventions

This referral does not meet the threshold for the directorate's involvement but you need to be aware that this information is now held on our records in respect of this incident.
Low level of concern letter

Children's Services have been notified by the police of an incident that occurred at your family home which falls under Domestic Violence protocols ... As you may be aware, the emotional impact of domestic violence is well researched and can be extremely harmful ... any further reports of this nature will likely result in a home visit being completed in order to discuss the next appropriate course of action.
High level of concern letter

(Stanley et al 2010b, p7)

In addition, letters were found to be ineffective in reducing the demands on children's services. The proportion of families who received letters as the sole form of intervention and who were re-referred or re-notified over the subsequent 21 months (55%) was slightly higher than the proportion of 'no further action' cases re-referred or re-notified (52%). The effect of letters on families is unpredictable and their threatening tone may well serve to reduce parents' motivation to engage with services; moreover, they do not appear to reduce the incidence of domestic violence in families.

Accountability and failure to protect

There are numerous accounts in research of social workers increasing pressure on women to leave abusive relationships by threatening legal proceedings in relation to the children. This punitive approach has been identified as a consequence of the failure of children's services to engage with abusive men (Humphreys 1999; D'Cruz 2002). In some US states, 'failure to protect' has been cited as grounds for care procedures in cases where mothers are perceived as unable or unwilling to leave their partners (Edleson 1998; Magen 1999; Johnson and Sullivan 2008). UK studies (Farmer and Owen 1995; Humphreys 1999; Stanley et al 2010c) have found evidence of a similar approach. In her study of child protection case conference minutes and plans Humphreys (1999) found that in a quarter of the 32 cases examined, mothers were warned at case conferences that if their abusive partner returned to the family home, legal interventions to remove the children would be implemented or case conferences would be reconvened. Stanley et al's (2010c) more recent study found that social workers were uncomfortable with this punitive approach, but a preoccupation with separation left them feeling they had few alternatives. This emphasis on separation is at odds with the evidence discussed in Chapter 2 of this review, which shows that domestic violence continues to be a risk to children post-separation in a high proportion of families.

Mothers are also likely to experience the interventions of the courts and court officers as coercive or threatening. The HMICA review (2005) of Cafcass's performance in relation to domestic violence included interviews with 30 mothers, as well as observation of 56 Cafcass interviews with parents. The inspectors found that Cafcass's work was dominated by a presumption of contact, which failed to acknowledge the impact of domestic violence on mothers and children, and that Cafcass practitioners failed to challenge abusive men. A US study offers a useful picture of families' experiences across both the legal and the child protection systems, and thus comes closer to capturing families' experiences of multiple institutions and interventions. Hulbert (2008) examined cases where children's experience of domestic violence resulted in court proceedings, collecting data from court and social services' records in four US states over four years. Her study included observation of court proceedings and surveys of victims and other stakeholders. She found that victims and batterers were not consistently identified and that management of the batterer, either through the criminal justice system or through provision of an intervention programme, was secondary to a focus on the victim's role as caregiver. Moreover, in common with Stanley et al's (2010c) study, Hulbert found that children were sometimes placed with a spouse or relative with a history of domestic violence.

Fostering trust and promoting disclosure in BME communities

An evaluation of Sure Start local programmes' work with parents experiencing domestic violence (Ball and Niven 2007) emphasises that domestic violence was most likely to be disclosed in the context of an ongoing trusting relationship with a practitioner. This was the case for all families receiving a Sure Start service. However, trust may be particularly difficult to establish with BME families who may feel excluded from mainstream services by language barriers and racism. Gray (2003) has described the work of the Family Support Service in Tower Hamlets where trust and disclosure of stigmatised issues such as domestic violence were fostered by cultural and linguistic matching of family support workers and Bangladeshi service users. Gray argues that support workers were able to offer appropriate and culturally sensitive interventions in the context of a close relationship that drew on a kinship model that allowed support workers to be identified as 'Auntie'. Staff required regular opportunities for supervision and reflection, which aimed to avoid risks of over-identification with families, as well as training in safety and child protection procedures and policies. Training and supervision are clearly key to the success of such interventions: the Sure Start evaluation (Ball and Niven 2007) noted that Asian Sure Start support workers originating from the same community as their clients could be reluctant to raise the issue of domestic violence, as exposing this issue to wider scrutiny might jeopardise their relationship with the local community.

Wilson (2010) charts the work of South Asian women's organisations in Britain, highlighting both their campaigning work on domestic violence and their role in establishing and providing refuges for South Asian women. She notes the success of these organisations in continuing to argue for and provide specialist services, despite continual shifts in the policy and funding landscape. Women and children participating in Mullender et al's (2002) research reported positive experiences of specialist Asian refuges. The researchers attributed this to the protection such services offered from racism and discrimination, as well as to the cultural and linguistic sensitivity of the refuges and their staff. However, a study of those using and providing domestic violence services in the Manchester area found that BME survivors of domestic violence reported conflicting pressures in relation to help-seeking within their own communities (Burman et al 2004). While disclosing abusive experiences to professionals outside their own community risked bringing that community into disrepute and made women vulnerable to racism, seeking support from organisations within their own community raised concerns about confidentiality. Women who had left violent partners feared being recognised and traced, and service providers acknowledged that small BME organisations dependent on local funders could be subjected to pressure from powerful individuals within the local community. A small-scale study with BME women working for one primary care trust (Wellock 2010) also found that women were anxious about disclosing domestic violence to professionals or interpreters from their own communities and feared that their confidentiality would not be protected.

In relation to forced marriages, Gangoli et al (2009) found that adult victims of child marriages were unlikely to see themselves as experiencing forced marriage and such perceptions would limit the likelihood of them seeking help. However, provision for victims of child marriage was also reported to be extremely scarce by organisations surveyed in this study.

Assessment

The Common Assessment Framework (CAF) was rolled out across England and Wales in 2006-08 with the aim of promoting early intervention in children's lives and engaging the full range of agencies in assessing and meeting children's needs. Research evidence on the impact of the CAF is still limited and, at the time of writing, there was little published material that addressed its use specifically in relation to children experiencing domestic violence. An early evaluation of the implementation of the CAF in Wales (Pithouse 2006) analysed children's services' records for 88 children aged up to nine following implementation. It compared the quality and extent of the information conveyed, as well as practice outcomes, with records prior to the implementation, and with those for a similar group of referrals in a comparison site. Analysis revealed that the most common reason for referral both before and after introduction of the CAF was neglect, and that domestic violence was one of the main factors associated with neglect, along with parental substance misuse and mental health needs. Domestic violence was also a key driver of referral. The amount of information concerning children's emotional and behavioural needs entered on referral forms was found to be relatively limited; the introduction of the CAF did not appear to have made a difference in this respect.

A study of early implementation of the CAF and the Lead Practitioner role in 12 trial sites in England (Brandon et al 2006) found that non-social care practitioners experienced a lack of skills and confidence in relation to asking families about complex issues such as domestic violence. Similarly, Adamson and Deverell's (2009) small-scale study of the implementation of the CAF in a rural setting found that teachers and pre-school workers who belonged to the same community as the families they worked with expressed discomfort about asking questions about domestic violence as part of the CAF procedure. Assessment and intervention with families in rural areas may need to take account of the tightly woven social networks and the sense of being open to public scrutiny that frequently characterise rural communities. Adamson and Deverell suggest that training and mentoring support may assist staff in this respect.

The extent of families' engagement with children's social care assessments appears variable. A study of children's social care interventions in families characterised by domestic violence and/or substance misuse (Cleaver et al 2007) found that only seven of the 17 families studied in depth were both aware that an assessment had been carried out and were informed about the plan developed from the assessment. These families described themselves as most fully involved in the process of assessment. A sense of involvement in the assessment process was associated with families' levels of satisfaction with the services they received. The research found that families and social workers were more likely to describe their relationship as good when families had agreed to the initial referral and where the relationship between family and social worker was experienced as positive, families were more likely to be honest with the social worker undertaking the assessment.

The HMICA review (2005) of Cafcass's performance in relation to domestic violence was critical of the 'narrative approach' taken in private law cases, which the inspectors concluded relied too heavily on reporting what was said rather than analysing and assessing the information collected. They found no evidence of risk assessments that addressed domestic violence, and safety planning was not undertaken. Cafcass practitioners were also found to be failing to give parents adequate information about the process of preparing a report and to engage with families on a partnership basis. Macdonald's (2010) study found while the risks posed by domestic violence and children's views did inform assessments, they were given less weight than other professional discourses, such as impartiality, agreement-seeking, the role of fathers and shared parenting. Although practitioners had responded to the recommendations of the HMICA review by addressing domestic violence in their reports, neutral language was often used and the perpetrator was not identified. Likewise, Baynes and Holland's (2010) analysis of 40 child protection case files in one English local authority identified numerous examples of sanitised language, which failed either to convey the seriousness of, or attribute responsibility for, domestic violence in social workers' accounts.

In the UK, Barnardo's have developed a tool known as the Domestic Violence Risk Identification Matrix, which is currently being used by children's social care practitioners in a number of London boroughs to inform assessments with families experiencing domestic violence. The matrix, which is based on a Canadian manual, was developed and implemented by Barnardo's in Northern Ireland (Bell and McGoren 2003). It classifies risks to children who are exposed to domestic violence at one of four thresholds, each of which is linked to a level of intervention. Information collected through the CAF is fed into the matrix and combined to produce one of four thresholds described in Box 6.4.

Box 6.4: The Domestic Violence Risk Identification Matrix

> Scale 1 (Moderate): This child(ren) and/or family are likely to need targeted support by a single practitioner.

> Scale 2 (Moderate to Serious): This child(ren) and/or family are likely to need integrated support by more than one agency, which should be co-ordinated by an identified lead professional.

> Scale 3 (Serious): Children's social services should consider Section 17 initial assessment, but safeguarding intervention may be necessary if threshold of significant harm is reached.

> Scale 4 (Severe): Children's social services should consider whether Section 47 enquiry and core assessment required.

(London Safeguarding Children Board 2008)

To date, evaluation of the Matrix has been confined to examining its implementation in three boroughs. Calder (2009) found practitioners reported that the Matrix was accessible and provided them with structure and detail they had previously lacked;

they felt it clarified thresholds and increased their confidence in decision-making. Reported difficulties included the lack of time available for practitioners to use the model, communication problems between agencies and problems with CAF implementation impacting on use of the Matrix.

Engaging with abusive fathers

There is considerable evidence that assessment processes tend to target mothers rather than abusive fathers. Stanley et al (2010b) reported that mothers in families experiencing domestic violence were more likely to be engaged in social work assessment and intervention than fathers. This pattern is characteristic of social care intervention in domestic violence: Humphreys (1999) found that men rarely participated in residential assessments while Holt's (2003) study of social work practice with families experiencing domestic violence in Ireland found a focus on women and an exclusion of men. Likewise, the evaluation of Sure Start intervention in domestic abuse (Ball and Niven 2007) found that Sure Start staff rarely engaged with perpetrators. An evaluation of two early intervention services in northern England (Donovan et al 2010) found that a wide range of practitioners in partner agencies, including children's services, were reluctant to engage with male perpetrators and did not consider this part of their remit. Practitioners saw work with perpetrators as being the responsibility of criminal justice agencies, which focused on the criminalisation of perpetrators rather than delivering interventions designed to change behaviour.

Stanley et al (2010b) found that the limited time frame for completing initial assessments militated against social workers engaging with male perpetrators; social workers in initial assessment teams were the least likely to see working with perpetrators of domestic violence as part of their role. Nor was other agencies' information on perpetrators always available to those completing initial assessments – for example, information from criminal records was not consistently communicated to children's services in police notification forms, although social workers found it valuable when it was. US guidance on child protection practice with families experiencing domestic violence (Bragg 2003) emphasises the value of incorporating information on the perpetrator's criminal history into the assessment.

A study of a sample of 40 child protection case files from one English local authority (Baynes and Holland 2010) found that two-thirds of the 63 men in the study had a recorded history of violence to women and children. Thirty-eight of the 63 men (60%) had no contact with a social worker prior to the initial child protection meeting and less than half were invited to attend the meeting, although all mothers were invited. Information about men's histories was not systematically collected. In common with Stanley et al's (2010b) study, in a third of cases no background check on men's criminal convictions appeared to have been undertaken.

A failure to engage abusive men in both assessment and intervention can be attributed to social work's focus on women and mothers (Scourfield 2003; Featherstone and Peckover 2007), but also to practitioners' experience or anticipation of perpetrators' intimidating or abusive behaviour (O'Hagan and Dillenburger 1995; Stanley 1997). A number of inquiries into child deaths have found that such fears have restricted the scope and depth of assessments and several studies have identified the psychological impact of service users' threats on practitioners (see Littlechild and Bourke 2006). Littlechild and Bourke (2006) argue that supervision is key to providing the opportunity for social workers to disclose fears of intimidation or aggression and that social care organisations need to have procedures that articulate how threatening or abusive service users will be managed. However, Baynes and Holland's (2010) local study found that while practitioners' levels of engagement with men generally were low, social workers visited men they considered to be violent at least as frequently as they did other men, and violent men were more likely than most men to be involved in all stages of the child protection process.

Practitioners' individual responses to perpetrators, victims and children may also be shaped by their own personal histories of domestic violence. A study of 303 children's social workers participating in domestic violence training in California found that personal experience of domestic violence and identification with the victim made social workers less likely to consider that it was effective to take children experiencing domestic violence into care (Yoshihama and Mills 2003). Less is known about how practitioners' individual histories might shape their readiness to engage with perpetrators and this is an area where further research might be useful. However, the studies identified here provide a strong argument for developing social workers' skills and confidence in working with abusive men.

Children's social care – patterns of engagement with families experiencing domestic violence

English et al (2000) studied outcomes for 1,263 cases of child abuse or neglect in Washington State, US, that were screened as not reaching the threshold for child protection services' intervention and which were diverted to a community-based, low-level intervention service. They found that the re-referral rate in the subsequent 18 months was highest for those families where domestic violence was identified as an issue. Some re-referrals were assessed as being at the severe end of the risk spectrum and the researchers conclude that families with a chronic history of domestic violence may require fuller assessment and more intrusive interventions. A later study by English et al (2005), which focused on the pathways taken by families through child protection services, found similarly high rates of re-referral for both low and high-risk domestic violence cases, and for those that received services as well as for those that did not. This study suggests that the interventions delivered were not sufficient to reduce the family's problems.

In England, Stanley et al's (2010b) study of children's services' interventions with families experiencing domestic violence identified a 'stop-start' approach in over a third of the cases followed up over 21 months. This took the form of a repeated pattern of assessments or short-term interventions that were withdrawn when couples appeared to separate, the perpetrator and/or the victim was judged to be addressing issues of substance misuse, or the perpetrator received a prison sentence. On occasion, reports of a separation proved at a later date to have been misleading and, as over 50 per cent of incidents included in the study sample involved separated couples, equating separation with safety seems inappropriate. This 'stop-start' approach to intervention appeared inadequate for effectively addressing complex family problems, which, in addition to domestic violence, often involved parental mental health needs, substance misuse and, for some families, behavioural or mental health problems in children or young people. In those cases where children entered the looked after system, homelessness was also identified as an issue. This stop-start approach was also evident in the pattern of intervention identified by Jones et al's (2002) Californian study, which found that families experiencing domestic violence were recycled through child protective services. Practitioners interviewed by Stanley et al (2010b) called for longer-term, more sustained interventions with families experiencing domestic violence:

'... these families need a lot longer, more targeted over time work.'

(Child protection manager, quoted in Stanley et al 2010b, p15)

Chapter six: Summary

> Recent research undertaken in the UK suggests that social care practitioners' understanding and awareness of domestic violence has increased substantially in the last decade.

> Screening for domestic violence has proved effective in promoting disclosure of domestic violence in a range of different settings. Relevant training appears to assist the implementation of routine enquiry.

> Children and young people report that they want professionals to talk to them about domestic violence, to keep them informed and to take their experiences and views seriously. Research exploring the practice of social workers appointed to produce reports for courts has found that they vary in the extent to which they talk directly with children about their experiences and acknowledge their involvement in domestic violence.

> In common with US and Australian states where professionals are mandated to refer families experiencing domestic violence to child protection services, police notifications of domestic violence incidents have produced a high volume of referrals to children's services in England and Wales. Only a small proportion of these notified cases receive a response from children's services. The majority receive a 'no further action' response, suggesting that early interventions need to be developed for this group.

> Letters sent to parents in families in lieu of any other intervention are ineffective in reducing the demands on children's services and in preventing children's exposure to domestic violence. They may also act to increase the risks of further abuse and reduce parents' motivation to engage with children's services.

> Mothers may experience intervention by children's services as coercive if they are threatened with legal proceedings as a consequence of a perceived failure to protect children from domestic violence. A practitioner focus on separation as the preferred outcome is likely to contribute to this sense of coercion. Victims of domestic violence are also likely to find courts and court officers threatening in their emphasis on maintaining contact and the lack of challenge or interventions for perpetrators.

> Disclosure of domestic violence is most likely to occur when children and families feel secure and can trust those in whom they are confiding. Trained specialist domestic violence staff and services have offered a means of providing these conditions to victims from BME communities, but services located in the same community as service users may also entail risks for BME victims.

> Evaluation of implementation of the Common Assessment Framework in England and Wales has suggested that education professionals may lack the skills and confidence required to raise the issue of domestic violence with families.

> Assessment processes tend to target mothers rather than fathers, who are less likely than mothers or children to be engaged in child protection procedures. Nor is information on perpetrators' criminal histories consistently available to children's social care assessments. Social workers' skills and confidence in working with abusive men need to be enhanced.

> High rates of re-referral to children's services for families experiencing domestic violence suggest that repeated stop-start interventions, which are curtailed when parents separate, are inadequate to deal with the long-term embedded problem that is domestic violence.

Chapter seven

The Service Response – Interventions

This chapter looks at the evidence base for the effectiveness of different types of service response intended to help children and families experiencing domestic violence. Specifically, this chapter examines the evidence for the effectiveness of:

> **different forms of early intervention, including parenting programmes, preventive programmes delivered to children in schools, community education programmes, and interventions for women and families vulnerable to domestic violence**

> **interventions to support children living with their mothers in refuges**

> **interventions targeted at mothers, including advocacy programmes and safety planning approaches**

> **programmes that deliver parallel support to mothers and their children (including the use of psychotherapeutic support and cognitive-behavioural therapy)**

> **perpetrator programmes, including court-directed programmes, community programmes and interventions that focus on the perpetrator's role as a father**

> **whole-family interventions, including Family Intervention Projects and use of the Family Group Decision Making approach.**

The chapter concludes with a short discussion of emerging models and tools designed to determine the cost-effectiveness of interventions by calculating the health, welfare, social and economic costs of domestic violence.

A summary of key findings is set out at the end of the chapter.

Previous chapters in this review have indicated which areas should be targeted by interventions for children and families experiencing domestic violence. A focus on mothers' mental health is key and the knowledge that mothers' parenting skills can be retrieved in the absence of domestic violence suggests the value of interventions that seek to repair and build parenting. Social support is also essential for mothers' mental health and can contribute to children's resilience. Ending children's exposure to domestic violence is clearly pivotal, but the last chapter reiterated the message that separation does not consistently signal an end to violence. It showed how easy it is for families to be recycled through children's services if separation is confused with the cessation of domestic violence. While separation may be an appropriate goal for some families, others will need intervention that accepts that parents will stay together or may be separated but nevertheless need to co-ordinate child contact arrangements. In these cases, the goal of intervention will be to end abusive behaviour, or at the very least to ensure that contact is safe and free of abuse, and this requires services to engage directly with fathers. It is also clear that children often lack a voice in key decisions and services need both to address this issue and to identify and intervene to meet the children's emotional, behavioural and health needs arising from exposure to domestic violence. For adolescents, there will be a need to identify and address violence and abuse in their own relationships.

While there are some examples of innovative interventions with children and families experiencing domestic violence in England and Wales, recent studies emphasise that the availability of interventions for children and their parents is patchy and generally insufficient to meet needs. Research with practitioners consistently reports a shortfall in therapeutic and other interventions for children exposed to domestic violence (Izzidien 2008; Robinson 2009; Stanley et al 2010c) as well as limited availability of perpetrator programmes (Stanley et al 2010c). It is, therefore, in part a reflection of the extent of service provision that the larger studies exploring the effectiveness of interventions cited in this chapter are again North American. A number of smaller local evaluations are available in the UK context. Although these are less reliable in their estimations of effectiveness, they do provide some useful suggestions for ways forward. This material may be particularly relevant for those planning and commissioning services in England and Wales.

Early interventions

MacMillan et al's (2009) review of interventions in child maltreatment notes the lack of evidence for interventions to prevent the onset of domestic violence. While there is an increasing body of evidence on the effectiveness of interventions to improve parenting, evidence is limited for the capacity of well-tested programmes – such as the Family Nurse Partnership or parenting-skills interventions such as Triple P or The Incredible Years – to impact on families' experience of domestic violence. The evaluation of the second year of the Family Nurse Partnership programme in England (Barnes et al 2009) found that, while domestic violence was one of the reasons families were referred to the service by social care agencies, there was no evidence that the programme's clients were experiencing less abuse from partners. The evaluation of the intervention in the US (Eckenrode et al, 2000) found that domestic violence constituted a barrier to client progress.

Barth (2009) examines the evidence for whether parenting programmes impact on child abuse. He notes that improving parenting skills, and directly addressing behaviours such as domestic violence that influence parenting skills, are two different approaches. His review suggests that more evidence is needed on whether parenting programmes can reduce child harm. He acknowledges that even if the Triple P programme, which combines community education with different levels of parenting training, was to be rolled out more widely, it would need to be complemented by interventions with families that directly address risk factors that contribute to child maltreatment, such as domestic violence.

Chapter 5 considered the evidence from some of the preventive programmes delivered directly to children and young people in schools in England and Wales. There have also been a range of public education programmes delivered to whole communities in the UK, some of which have been supported by the Zero Tolerance Charitable Trust, while others have been funded by local authorities and health trusts. These campaigns aim to raise awareness, provide information and connect victims and perpetrators to relevant community resources (see Ellis 2008 and Stanley et al 2009 for a fuller discussion of such campaigns). While broadly targeted campaigns that harness the media and a range of advertising techniques have the capacity to increase public awareness and knowledge of domestic violence, the link between such attitudinal change and behaviour change is not well established (Harvey et al 2007). In their review of domestic violence public education campaigns, Donovan and Vlais (2005) argue that pre-campaign research demonstrates public awareness of domestic violence is generally high and they suggest that public education campaigns should be carefully targeted on particular groups, such as victims or perpetrators.

The Freedom Programme is a preventive intervention that targets women vulnerable to domestic violence. It aims to enable participants to recognise abusive behaviour from current or ex-partners and to identify its effects on themselves and their children. This 12-week group programme has a rolling intake and is delivered by a network of trained and licensed practitioners across the UK, including staff in some children's centres (Ball and Niven 2007). In their evaluation of the Freedom Programme in Bristol, Williamson and Abrahams (2010) found that two-thirds of the 31 women participating in the research were no longer in a relationship at the time of accessing the programme; however, 20 reported that their previous partner had been aggressive towards them. At the outset of the programme, women's confidence, self-esteem and contentment were low. Unfortunately, the follow-up engaged only a small number of participants and although their reports were positive, a larger-scale evaluation is required to capture the impact of this programme.

Safe Start in Spokane, Washington, US, represents an early intervention service targeted on families who do not reach the threshold for intervention from child protection services. The service adopted a crisis-intervention model and aimed to engage in short-term interventions those families who were experiencing domestic violence and had a child aged under six. Referrals came primarily from law-enforcement agencies and were managed by a team of qualified practitioners providing a round-the-clock service and responding within 24 hours of an incident. Interventions were designed to:

> establish immediate and ongoing safety

> identify resources and practical actions to increase physical and emotional comfort

> reduce emotional distress

> identify short and long-term needs to guide extended support

> empower individuals to use existing coping skills

> connect families to relevant resources and agencies.

(Blodgett et al 2008, p78)

The evaluation (Blodgett et al 2008) utilised data from records kept by practitioners delivering the service to identify outcomes for the 270 children and their families accessing the service. Benefits such as improved functioning for adults and children, reduced emotional distress, increased use of relevant services and ending the violent relationship were identified for 13 per cent of children and families. Such outcomes were most likely to be found in the small group of 26 children and their families who had experienced more than five direct contacts with the service. These findings may, in part, be an artefact of the way in which evidence of impact was collected – more evidence was likely to have been available on families with whom there had been most contact. However, they also suggest that very brief interventions may be less effective for families experiencing domestic violence.

In the UK, Donovan et al (2010) evaluated two pilot projects in the north of England that provided an early intervention service to victims, perpetrators and children. Box 7.1 provides details of the services and the evaluation, which took place between 2004 and 2009 and involved 56 interviews with victims/survivors using the service, interviews with staff and managers, and analysis of quantitative data from the projects' own databases and from the police and Crown Prosecution Service.

Box 7.1: Safer Families, Gateshead, and Letgo, Cumbria

Service characteristics

> Two projects – one urban (Gateshead), one rural (Cumbria) – funded by the Northern Rock Foundation to provide an early intervention service.

> Services located within multiagency partnerships (provided by domestic violence forum/ partnership/strategic management board) to facilitate multiagency work.

> Services provided co-ordination, advocacy and caseworking.

> Staffed by IDVAs and children's workers.

> Referrals received from the police following domestic violence incidents – Cumbria also accepted referrals from other agencies and self-referrals.

> In Gateshead, victims/survivors 'opted in' to the service (ie gave consent for referral to service); in Cumbria, victims/survivors 'opted out' (ie officers made a referral unless victim/survivor declined).

> Contact with survivor/victim within 24 hours, early risk assessment to develop and implement safety plan.

> Individual and group work provided to children.

> Voluntary perpetrator programmes.

Evaluation findings:

> The services were successful in reducing repeat referrals and reports of incidents; the majority of victims/survivors were assessed as being at reduced risk following engagement with the projects and victims/ survivors' own perceptions of risk were reduced.

> Victims/survivors described themselves as having been helped to recognise their experiences as domestic violence and as more confident in seeking help.

> Victims/survivors with complex needs were less likely to experience risk reduction, and required more input and longer periods of engagement to achieve change.

> The services for children appeared to be filling a gap in provision – criticisms related to waiting times and availability; however, the impact of the services on children was not assessed.

> The projects were less successful in their work with perpetrators – the proportion of cases progressing through the courts remained low and the numbers signing up for perpetrator programmes were limited.

> Both projects encountered challenges regarding multiagency working, including:

> > difficulties in establishing credibility with other agencies

> > difficulties in achieving sufficiently senior management representation on strategic boards

> > problems in communication and information sharing with other agencies.

> Multiagency engagement fell away over time leaving a hard core of criminal justice, housing and children's agencies. One project had more success in maintaining engagement of other agencies as a result of addressing agency roles and mechanisms for co-ordination early in its planning stages (see Chapter 8 for a fuller discussion of such approaches).

(Donovan et al 2010)

Interventions with children in refuges

Most refuges provide services for children. However, there has been little research on this topic and, with the exception of Mullender et al's (1998) UK study, there has been limited evaluation of these interventions (Poole et al 2008). While many refuges in England and Wales employ children's workers, limitations in funding and space have been identified as imposing restrictions on the interventions offered to children (Izzidien 2008; Wilson 2010). Although the brevity of a child's stay in a refuge may further reduce opportunities for intervention, a refuge stay can also be conceptualised as a key opportunity for a child's need for support to be assessed and the family put in contact with relevant services. Webb et al (2001) assessed the health of 147 children in Cardiff refuges. They found that 30 per cent of those screened had delayed immunisations, 19 per cent per cent were assessed as having delayed or questionable development and 48 per cent had mental health difficulties. The researchers conclude that these children had a high level of health needs and that frequent moves had resulted in limited access to services. A refuge stay is therefore a window of opportunity for children's needs to be assessed and treatment and support instigated.

Children and young people who took part in Mullender et al's (2002) UK research described wanting a refuge to provide activities that 'took you out of yourself' while also offering occasions to share experiences of domestic violence:

'Someone to trust – a nice environment, homely, that will raise their confidence. Toys and games to occupy their time. Someone to talk to them about what they are feeling and to help them understand why it is better that they have left ... You need people to understand how you are feeling and help you to cope with the changes.'

(14-year-old South Asian boy, quoted in Mullender et al 2002, p102)

Key interventions offered by refuges are listed in Box 7.2.

Box 7.2: Interventions for children offered by refuges

> structured play which may be used to learn and practice coping skills and may include expression through art

> storytelling to offer empathy and demonstrate problem solving

> music, dance and drama which also offer opportunities to learn new skills and to express feelings

> individual counselling

> groups that offer opportunities for children to share their experiences of domestic violence

> assistance with transition to new schools

> child advocacy.

Mullender et al's (1998) research found that refuges were offering a number of these interventions. However, refuge workers participating in their study reported difficulties in providing appropriate activities for teenagers and noted that some older boys could represent a disruptive male presence in refuges. Staff were also concerned to ensure that refuges had the facilities and attitudes for responding to the needs of both disabled children and black children.

Tyndall-Lind et al (2001) compared the effects of an intensive programme of 12 sessions of sibling play therapy delivered to ten children (aged four to nine) in US refuges with a similar programme delivered on an individual basis to children in refuges. The study employed a control group who received neither intervention. In contrast to the control group, mothers' reports showed a marked improvement in behaviour problems in both groups of children receiving the play therapy; aggressive behaviour was significantly reduced. The researchers argue that although the behavioural measures used showed no differences between those receiving individual and sibling play therapy, the sibling therapy served to decrease feelings of secrecy and isolation and allowed for the creation of positive family dynamics that could be re-enacted outside therapy. However, this study also demonstrates some of the challenges of delivering interventions to children in refuges: 20 children were originally recruited to participate in sibling therapy, but ten left the refuge before they could complete the sessions.

Contact services

As noted earlier in this review, children will vary in their views about whether they wish to maintain contact with abusive fathers following separation (Peled 1998; Harrison 2006). UK courts and Cafcass officers have been criticised for the presumption of contact that informs their decisions and reports (Radford and Hester 2006; HMICA 2005), and the previous chapter noted that children's views on contact are not consistently sought by social workers and CAFCASS officers. However, many mothers and children will seek to maintain contact with abusive fathers following separation. Chapter 4 of this review identified a range of ways in which contact has been used as a means to perpetuate abuse of both women and children.

Professionally supervised contact is a limited resource in England and Wales. A lot of contact is either unsupervised or poorly supervised by friends or family (Radford and Hester 2006). A study of the work of supported and supervised contact centres in England and Wales (Harrison 2006) found that in most supported contact centres, supervision of contact took the form of observation from a distance; less than half the centres had separate exits and entrances, which would have facilitated the separation of victim and perpetrator. Over half the centres did not undertake safety or risk assessments, even when domestic violence was known to be a factor, and the researchers found that the terms 'supported' and supervised' did not mean the same thing to the professionals, centre staff and parents involved, resulting in confusion and ambiguity.

Interventions for mothers

Chapter 4 noted the role of social support in mediating mothers' capacity to parent, both while they are living with domestic violence and once they have left an abusive situation. Advocacy has increasingly been identified as the means by which women can be assisted to access the social and community resources needed to rebuild independent lives for themselves and their children. Sullivan and Bybee's (1999) US study of advocacy support for women who had been accommodated in shelters is unusual in its use of a randomised control group. The researchers randomly allocated 143 of the 278 women in their sample to an advocacy programme delivered over 10 weeks, which focused on devising a safety plan and mobilising community resources. Women were interviewed six times over the two-year period subsequent to using the shelter. The findings provided strong evidence for the value of the intervention: women who reported wanting to end their relationship at their first interview were more likely to do so if they had received the advocacy service; women in receipt of the service accessed relevant resources more quickly; and at six-month follow-up, physical violence and depression were significantly lower in the advocacy group, while social support and quality of life were significantly higher. Over the following two years, those women who had received advocacy services continued to report higher levels of social support and quality of life, and less depression. One in four women in the advocacy group experienced no further violence in the 24-month follow-up period, compared to one in ten in the control group.

Sullivan and Bybee's study has been influential in the development of the Independent Domestic Violence Advisors (IDVAs) service in England and Wales. This crisis-focused service provides short to medium-term support to women judged to be at high risk of domestic violence and also aims to co-ordinate the delivery of relevant services. The early evaluation (Howarth et al 2009) of seven of these services found that 57 per cent of women who received an IDVA service over a period of approximately four months experienced a cessation of abuse during that period. Although IDVAs do not work directly with children, the evaluation found evidence to suggest that women with children received a priority service from IDVAs. Victims with children were more likely to receive safety planning and to have their cases referred to a Multi-Agency Risk Assessment Conference (MARAC). At termination of the service, fears about the impact of domestic violence on children had reduced substantially. The proportions of mothers concerned about their former partners' threats to kill children, or about conflict over contact, were almost halved and fears of harm to children from former partners were also reduced by 76 per cent. An additional study (Robinson 2009) evaluating the implementation of IDVA services in four sites emphasised the need for IDVAs to maintain their independence and recommended that they should be organised into teams managed by specialist domestic violence services, which could increase their access to clinical supervision.

Safety planning

Safety planning is a commonly used approach with women experiencing domestic violence that developed in refuges and constitutes a component of the work undertaken by specialist domestic violence police officers, refuges and IDVAs. While most advocates of this approach emphasise that safety planning should be based on women's own understanding of their needs and situation, safety plans are likely to include some of the measures listed in Box 7.3.

Box 7.3: Safety plan components

> Identifying a safe place in case of further violence

> Awareness of safe personal contacts

> Procedures for contacting helpline and emergency services

> Security measures for the home, eg locks, panic buttons and alarms

> Keeping important documents in a safe and secure place

> Maintaining a cache of spare keys, money and emergency clothing.

(Hester et al 2007)

Although safety planning is widely used in the UK, this review did not identify any UK evaluations of its effectiveness. However, a US study evaluated the delivery of safety planning to 132 pregnant women who had experienced domestic violence across a period of a year (McFarlane et al 1998). Each woman received three nurse-delivered sessions that involved review of the perpetrator's behaviour and discussion and development of a safety plan. The evaluation showed a substantial rise in the women adopting a range of safety measures across pregnancy and in the 12 months following birth, with a significant increase in women's safety behaviours taking place following the initial session. This intervention, like others delivered in pregnancy such as the Family Nurse Partnership, may derive some of its effectiveness from mothers' high levels of motivation to seek and use support during pregnancy.

In her critique of risk assessment and management approach for women experiencing domestic violence, Hoyle (2008) argues that an expectation that victims will act on the recommendations of the personal safety plan developed by the police puts women in a position where they can be held individually accountable for reducing the risk of further violence, making them vulnerable to blame. She suggests that while some women experience safety plans as empowering, others find that the costs of the restrictions imposed by such plans are too high –15 of the 35 safety plans she studied suggested substantial life changes, such as switching children's schools, routes to work or working patterns. She notes that women trade off the risks posed by domestic violence against other risks in their lives and may therefore choose not to implement such plans.

Some of the programmes delivered to children, such as the Sutton Stronger Families Programme described below, incorporate a form of safety planning aimed specifically at children. Such plans are likely to include identifying a trusted adult elsewhere who can be contacted in a dangerous situation, calling for help, finding a safe place in the case of violence and not intervening in violent incidents (Mullender 1996). Again, although this approach is increasingly used with children, it does not appear to have been evaluated in the UK. However, an evaluation (Ernst et al 2008) was undertaken in Albuquerque, New Mexico, where the Child Witness to Violence Program involved play, art, pet therapy and safety planning. The programme varied in length according to the child's assessed needs and an overall goal was for children to learn they were not responsible for the violence. Of the 58 children aged between 3 and 17 who participated in the evaluation, 36 per cent improved their ability to use a safety plan, 41 per cent extended their knowledge of what to do during a violent episode and 36 per cent increased their ability to identify a safe adult by the end of the programme. The reliability of these findings is open to question, however, given that the evaluations were undertaken by the social workers delivering the programme. Nevertheless, they suggest that children were able to absorb and use the key principles of safety planning. This is consistent with Mullender et al's (2002) UK research with children and young people, which found that some children experiencing domestic violence were spontaneously using and developing their own safety planning strategies.

Interventions with mothers and children

Increasingly, services are aimed at both mothers and children, with interventions either being delivered to them both together or with parallel interventions being offered by one service. A US study offers evidence to support this approach (Graham-Bermann et al 2007). The researchers randomly allocated a third of 212 children (aged 6 to 12) and their mothers who had experienced domestic violence to one of two groups: (i) a 10-week group programme for children only; (ii) the children's group programme and a parallel group for mothers aimed at improving their parenting, including their ability to talk to their children about experiences of violence. The remaining third of the sample were placed on a waiting list. Children's attitudes and levels of aggression were most likely to improve when both mother and child received a service. Those children receiving the children's group intervention only showed no difference following intervention in their attitudes and behavioural problems from those children on the waiting list. Interestingly, a quarter of the children who were allocated to the waiting list only showed a spontaneous improvement in their aggressive externalising behaviour over the course of the study. Although the study has some limitations – the research relied on mothers' reports on their children's behaviours and these may have been influenced by participation in the parenting groups – it does provide evidence for the value of strengthening parenting as a means of reinforcing interventions delivered directly to children.

In the UK, this model of concurrent interventions for mothers and children experiencing domestic violence is used by the Sutton Stronger Families Programme. Established in 2003, the service is housed within the London Borough of Sutton Children and Families Service and is funded by the local authority, the primary care trust and the Children's Fund. The group programme for children experiencing domestic violence and the concurrent programme for their mothers was developed in Ontario, Canada; in the UK the programme is in the process of being duplicated in Nottingham and in London. The co-ordinator works with a team of co-facilitators whose time is contributed to the programme by their employer agencies. The key components of the programme are identified in Box 7.4.

Box 7.4: Sutton Stronger Families Group Programme

Referrals: Children and their mothers are referred to the service by a range of agencies and mothers can also refer directly; most children and their mothers are referred from children's services or schools. All children and their mothers receive an individual assessment.

Concurrent groups for children and their mothers: The service provides a range of closed groups for children and young people, each lasting 12 weeks; different groups cater for children from different age bands. Concurrent groups are run for mothers whose children are using the service.

The aims of the children's groups are to:

> help children to understand what domestic violence is and that it is not their fault

> plan safety strategies for themselves if it happens again

> deal with loss and change in a safe environment

> help children to move on from the situation.

The aims of the concurrent group for mothers are to:

> help them to be able to reinforce the messages the children are learning on their programme

> develop strategies for helping their children to be safe from and recover from domestic violence

> assist them to take care of themselves as survivors of abuse in that process.

(Debbonaire 2007)

The programme has been independently evaluated (Debbonaire 2007) and although this was not a 'before and after' evaluation, it produced some useful indications of the intervention's effectiveness. The need for careful assessment procedures was emphasised by the finding that approximately one in three children referred to the service were either assessed as unsuitable or did not need the service when it was offered. However, 37 of the 46 children who entered groups over a period of 18 months completed a 12-week programme. Children who were interviewed about their experiences of the programme felt they had found out about domestic violence and had learned that it was wrong and not their fault. They had also discovered they were not alone in their experiences of domestic violence and were more able to deal with their feelings and to communicate about their experiences:

'I learnt how to communicate better.' 'I learnt how to control my anger and see things from other people's points of view.' 'I learnt that it's OK to talk.'

(Children quoted in Debbonaire 2007, p3)

Bunston (2008) describes a similar initiative that developed from a collaboration between child mental health and community health services in Victoria, Australia. The Parents Accepting Responsibility that Kids are Safe (PARKAS) programme uses the same team of facilitators to run both a mothers' group and a group for children aged 8 to 12. Activities in the children's group are replicated in the mothers' group and this facilitates mothers' engagement with their child's perspective on domestic violence and family relationships. For instance, when children are asked to draw a family picture, mothers are asked to draw what they imagine their child would draw. The Peek a Boo Club is a parallel group intervention for mothers and infants up to 36 months. Again, the group setting is used as a means to encourage mothers to observe and identify their baby's emotional responses and to consider how exposure to domestic violence may be shaping their development. While the intervention for infants has not yet been evaluated, there is some evidence for the impact of the PARKAS programme on family difficulties scores. The value of harnessing new mothers' receptivity to interventions is highlighted:

> Hopefulness in creating a new future for their baby and thus
> for themselves, is vividly apparent.
>
> (Bunston 2008, p338)

It was noted in Chapter 4 that the transition from refuge accommodation to new housing can be difficult for mothers and children as new demands are likely to be experienced in a context of reduced support. McDonald et al (2006) evaluated the impact of the US Project SUPPORT intervention designed for women attempting to establish households independent of their abusive partners and who had at least one child with conduct problems that merited a clinical diagnosis. The intervention had two components: social and instrumental support for mothers similar to that offered by the advocacy service evaluated by Sullivan and Bybee (1999) and discussed above; and a parenting skills component. Weekly sessions of 60 to 90 minutes were offered for up to eight months following departure from the refuge. Women and children participating in the intervention were followed up 24 months after the intervention had ended. Although numbers of families taking part in the evaluation were small – 13 engaged with Project SUPPORT and 17 in the control arm receiving existing services – the evaluation provided evidence of fewer children with clinical levels of behaviour problems in the intervention group, fewer mothers reporting using aggressive child management strategies and fewer mothers returning to their abusive partners in the 24-month follow-up period. Such findings emphasise the importance of providing follow-up support in the period when mothers are attempting to build independent lives for themselves and their children following domestic violence.

In the UK, Humphreys et al (2006a) developed the Talking to my Mum intervention, which focuses on repairing communication between mothers and children. They highlight the 'conspiracy of silence' that surrounds domestic violence, even within the child-mother relationship. They describe how this silence is perpetuated by children and mothers' mutual concerns to protect one another, and by mothers' often mistaken beliefs that children are unaware of the abuse. The intervention, developed through an action research project, consists of activity packs (Humphreys et al 2006b and 2006c) designed for two different age groups (five to eight-year-olds and over-nines), which mothers and children work through together. While one activity pack is intended for the use of children and mothers living in refuge accommodation, another is designed for use in community settings. Early evaluation (Humphreys et al 2006a) found that the materials did evoke positive responses from families but noted also that some mothers needed support from refuge workers, both to acknowledge the extent to which their children had been exposed to and affected by the violence and to manage children's responses when open communication was established. A longitudinal study of the experiences of 23 women who had used refuges in England (Abrahams 2007) found that those with children were ready to accept advice on parenting matters from refuge staff.

Psychotherapy represents a more intensive form of intervention for mothers and children. In the US, Lieberman et al (2005) studied the effects of child-parent psychotherapy for mothers and their pre-school children who had experienced domestic violence. Seventy-five mother and child dyads were randomly assigned to either the psychotherapy programme or to case management with included referral to individual treatment in the community. The children assigned to the child-parent psychotherapy intervention showed significantly less behaviour problems and traumatic stress disorder symptoms at the conclusion of a 50-week treatment programme than the children in the control group. The researchers interpret this as an increase in mothers' capacity for responsiveness, accompanied by a growth in the child's trust in the mother's capacity to offer protective care. Mothers participating in child-parent psychotherapy also showed significantly fewer PTSD avoidance symptoms than mothers in the control group.

Cognitive behavioural therapy (CBT) is increasingly being advocated as an intervention for PTSD. Cohen and Mannarino (2008) describe a trauma-focused CBT programme for children and parents that provides training in stress management skills as preparation for direct discussion and processing of children's traumatic experiences. The intervention involves both individual sessions for parents and children and joint sessions where children share the 'trauma narratives' they have produced with their suitably prepared parent. This approach has been successfully used with children who have experienced sexual abuse and who have been exposed to disasters such as the New York terrorist attacks. It is currently being trialled for children who have experienced domestic violence.

In England and Wales, psychotherapeutic interventions with children experiencing domestic violence are most likely to be delivered by child and adolescent mental health services (CAMHS). However, this review uncovered little evidence relating to CAMHS interventions in this field.

Interventions with abusive men/fathers

While there is a substantial body of evidence on interventions for perpetrators of domestic violence, it is only quite recently that their role as fathers have been taken on board either by interventions or in programme evaluations. Programmes for male perpetrators were established earlier in North America than in the UK and much of the evidence base for programme effectiveness is therefore drawn from there. From 2003 onwards, the probation service in England and Wales rolled out the Integrated Domestic Abuse Programme (IDAP) and the Community Domestic Violence Programme (CDVP); both use cognitive behavioural approaches, with the IDAP programme based on the model developed in Duluth, Minnesota, and the CDVP drawing on an initiative delivered by the Canadian Correctional Service. These programmes are exclusively for perpetrators mandated to attend by the criminal courts following a conviction for a domestic violence offence. (A small number of prisons deliver the Healthy Relationships Programme, which does not comprise part of an offender's sentence.) An early evaluation of the implementation of the pilot IDAP programmes is available (Bilby and Hatcher 2004) and Bullock et al (2010) examined programme process and risk assessment across all these types of programme, but there is as yet limited evidence on the programmes' effectiveness since community programmes have not succeeded in collecting sufficient pre- and post-programme measures to inform such an evaluation.

Additional perpetrator programmes have been established in the UK by voluntary sector organisations or through voluntary-statutory sector partnerships. Such programmes take self-referrals with some also taking referrals from the courts and children's services. Some of these voluntary programmes have been independently evaluated (Burton et al 1998; Bell and Stanley 2005; ADVA and Sue Penna Associates 2009; Williamson and Hester 2009), although the ability to generalise from such evaluations is limited by the small numbers involved and the high drop-out rate from both the programmes and the research. However, Respect, the independent organisation that accredits and supports perpetrator programmes, has commissioned a multi-site evaluation of community-based perpetrator programmes in the UK. This is scheduled to report in 2012 (Debbonaire 2010).

Both the IDAP and CDVP programmes, as well as the various voluntary programmes available, offer support services for partners of programme participants, with the aim of monitoring perpetrators' progress while also providing support for their partners. However, Bullock et al's (2010) study noted that communication between women's safety workers and those managing the offender was not always of a consistent quality or sufficiently timely, and that women's safety workers could be marginalised within programmes.

Gondolf (2002; 2004) undertook a large-scale US evaluation of perpetrator programmes over four sites over seven years, involving 840 men and their partners. His evaluation found that programme participation was more effective in ending men's violence than criminal justice sanctions and that the majority of men participating in programmes had not re-assaulted their partner four years after the programme. The effects of participation in programmes increased over time, with the highest rate for re-assaults taking place in the first six months of the evaluation and the rate of re-assaults reducing after that. At follow-up, which took place 30 and 48 months after programme commencement, over two-thirds of participants' partners reported that their quality of life had improved and 85 per cent felt very safe (Gondolf 2004). Gondolf (2000) found that men mandated by the courts were more likely to change their behaviour than self-referrals and argued for their attendance on programmes to be closely monitored, with sanctions applied if necessary by the courts. His evaluation suggests that integrating programmes into a co-ordinated community response to domestic violence contributes to better outcomes. This evaluation (Gondolf 2004) also identifies a need to focus on programme intensity rather than length.

In the UK, Dobash et al (1999) evaluated two Scottish perpetrator programmes for men mandated to attend by the courts. They used reports from programme participants and their partners, as well as reoffending figures, to compare the outcomes for these men with those for a group subject to other criminal justice sanctions, such as fines, admonishments, probation and imprisonment. At follow-up 12 months after the initial interview, 66 per cent of the men participating in the programmes had remained violence free, while only 30 per cent of those in the control group had done so. The partners of men participating in the programme were also significantly less likely to report frequent violence.

While the findings from these large-scale evaluations are encouraging, it is apparent that some men participating in programmes do reoffend. Sartin et al's (2006) review of perpetrator programmes identifies a need for follow-up interventions subsequent to participation in programmes and suggests that methods for reinforcing and sustaining behaviour change outside the context of a group programme need to be developed. Box 7.5 summarises findings from research that has provided rigorous evaluation of perpetrator programmes.

> **Box 7.5: Key findings from perpetrator programmes evaluations**
>
> > Perpetrator programmes have been shown to be successful in reducing men's violence for the majority of men who attend.
>
> > They improve the quality of life and safety for the majority of participants' partners.
>
> > Given that a proportion of participants will reoffend, follow-up interventions should be offered.
>
> > Programme intensity appears to be more significant than programme length.
>
> > Programmes should be linked in to a range of other community responses to domestic violence.

Little has been written about work with BME perpetrators in the UK. Guru (2006) argues that perpetrator programmes in the UK have marginalised the specific needs of black and Asian men. He suggests that they draw on Canadian models of work with Asian men (Almeida and Dolan-Delvecchio 1999) to develop approaches that explore the influence of culture, history and politics on South Asian men's abusive behaviour.

As programmes in England and Wales are expanding, participation in perpetrator programmes is increasingly being identified by children's social care as a means of intervention in families where children are exposed to domestic violence. Debbonaire (2010, p3) suggests that 'social services are now effectively operating a mandate for programme attendance' whereby abusive men are directed to attend programmes as a means of acquiring access to their children or avoiding care proceedings. An evaluation of the South Tyneside Domestic Abuse Perpetrator Programme (Williamson and Hester 2009) found that a high proportion of referrals to this service came from children's social care. Although some men took an instrumental approach to programme participation, the 18 men interviewed identified a range of benefits as a result of participating in the programme and the majority of partners of programme participants interviewed were also positive about the programme.

Similarly, the evaluation of the East London DVIP (Price et al 2009), a service which is jointly commissioned by the London Boroughs of Barking and Dagenham, Newham and Waltham Forest, found that approximately two-thirds of the referrals to the perpetrators' programme came from children's services. The evaluators' claims for the service's effectiveness in reducing repeat victimisation rates require more detailed supporting evidence, but the majority of social workers commenting on the service's assessments of perpetrators found these very useful. Similarly, 78 per cent of social workers surveyed assessed children's safety as much improved following DVIP intervention (Price et al 2009).

Increasingly, in a context of referrals from or men's involvement with children's social care services, perpetrator programmes are addressing men's roles as fathers. The Caring Dads programme – developed in Ontario, Canada, and subsequently established in Swansea, Flintshire, Trafford and London in the UK – takes abusive men's role as fathers as its explicit focus. The UK evaluation is currently in process but the findings of the early Canadian evaluation (Scott and Crooks 2007) of this 17-week group programme are available. Men attending this programme had been identified as abusive to their children and/or their partners and were referred by child protection services and a range of other criminal justice, health and community organisations; the service emphasises the need for good communication and feedback to referring organisations. The service also received a small number of self-referrals. The majority of men attended the programme reluctantly: of 105 men referred to Caring Dads in its second year of operation, only 42 completed an intake session and attended at least one group session; however, 34 of these completed the entire programme. Pre- and post-intervention assessment of 23 participants in the programme found that fathers' hostility, denigration and rejection towards their children, as well as their level of angry arousal to child and family situations, decreased following the programme. Men's stress levels also decreased. However, this evaluation was undertaken by individuals involved in developing the programme and therefore lacked independence. It also did not have access to reports on participants' behaviour from referring agencies (Scott and Crooks 2007). Nevertheless, it provides useful evidence of an intervention that seeks to close the gap identified in Chapter 4 of this review between men as perpetrators of domestic violence and men as fathers.

Whole-family interventions

The use of Family Group Conferences (FGCs) with families experiencing domestic violence has been controversial, with some critics claiming that men's power and control behaviour does not get addressed in the context of the FGC (see Lupton and Nixon 1999). However, Pennell and Burford (2000) describe the use of Family Group Decision Making (FGDM) in eastern Canada with 32 families; their study utilised a comparison group selected from child protection case files. Comparison of file data showed that maltreatment was reduced among children in the FGDM group and abusive events declined for mothers in the FGDM group while they rose for mothers in the comparison group. Child-to-adult abuse was also reduced in the FGDM group, although it continued in four FGDM families and emerged in a fifth family subsequent to the FGC. The researchers suggest that one factor contributing to the success of FGDM in this evaluation was the basic premise that no family member should be victimised or should victimise other members.

This model has been implemented in the UK by the Daybreak Dove Programme; it was established first in Basingstoke and now in Bournemouth/Poole and in Portsmouth. This multiagency initiative takes referrals from statutory and voluntary agencies, with some programmes also accepting self-referrals from families. Programme staff suggest that the use of FGCs serves to erode the secrecy that traditionally surrounds domestic violence. Internal evaluations indicate that the programme has had some success in reducing families' contact with the local police subsequent to the intervention (Hampshire Constabulary 2007 and 2010).

A whole-family approach is a key feature of the work of the Family Intervention Projects (FIPs), 53 of which were established in England in 2006-07. The early evaluation (White et al 2008) identified domestic violence as a feature in 25 per cent of the families characterised by high levels of antisocial behaviour who received FIP services. At the point where families left FIPs, antisocial behaviour and criminal activities had reduced and interviews with staff and children and families captured reports of improved outcomes for children in the form of improved health, increased confidence, reduced self-harm and addiction behaviours, improvements in school attendance and participation in education and employment. The key features of FIPs contributing to a high-quality service are shown in Box 7.6.

> **Box 7.6: Key features of Family Intervention Projects contributing to success**
>
> > Recruitment and retention of high-quality staff – this allowed interventions to take place in the context of trusting relationships.
>
> > Small caseloads – this facilitated an 'intensity' that enabled deeply entrenched problems to be explored fully and ensured a persistency and availability to respond to crises.
>
> > Key worker model – this acted to secure families' engagement, trust and motivation.
>
> > Whole-family approach – this enhanced capacity to get to the root of the problem and to shift entrenched behaviour and attitudes within a family.
>
> > Staying involved with a family for as long as necessary – a 'long-haul' approach allowed time for relationships to be built.
>
> > Scope to use resources creatively – a flexible approach allowed for services to be bought in and resources to be tailored to families' needs.
>
> > Using sanctions with support – the possibility of sanctions being applied assisted families to acknowledge the need for behavioural change and increased motivation.
>
> > Effective multiagency work – this sent a consistent message to families, enabled the FIPs to get to the root of the problem and ensured that families received relevant services.
>
> (White et al 2008)

Although this early evaluation of the work of the FIPs focused on process rather than outcomes, these key features offer the outline of a strategy for addressing behaviour and attitudes that are deeply embedded in families and communities. Domestic violence is one such issue. The approach described is both broad and deep: broad in that it addresses all family members and is sustained over time, and deep in that it offers a high amount of worker-family contact, which creates a safe and trusting relationship in which hidden problems can be exposed and addressed.

A response of this nature contrasts with the stop-start pattern of the children's services' response to domestic violence described in the previous chapter. That could be characterised as a 'shallow' response that fails to acknowledge the embedded nature of domestic violence in families and does not permit the construction of safe trusting relationships within which abusive behaviour can be disclosed, acknowledged by all family members and addressed. A sustained and deep intervention will be required if perpetrators are to recognise their behaviour as domestic violence or abuse, if the impact of domestic violence on children is to be acknowledged by both parents, and if the abusive behaviour is to change or children's safety is to be achieved through separation.

Services for vulnerable groups

Women in the UK with no recourse to public funds face heightened barriers to accessing support services for themselves and their children. One study reported the difficulties experienced by 30 South Asian women who were barred from accessing public funds because their relationship with their partner had broken down as a consequence of domestic violence within two years of their arrival in the UK (Anitha 2010). The research, undertaken in North-West England, found that children's services used Section 20 of the Children Act 1989 to support women who had children, but the nature and extent of the services they received varied, with some women only receiving financial support or offers of accommodation for the children alone. Support from children's services was often the means by which women accessed legal services. Isolation was a particular feature of the experience of this group of families, particularly when mothers lacked access to specialist services that provided interpreters. Access to refuges was limited for this group but refuge provision, particularly when provided by specialist refuges serving the BME community, was valued when it was available.

The Sojourner Project, a pilot project funded by the Home Office and run by Eaves from 2009 to 2011, funded refuges providing accommodation and support for women and children who were victims of domestic violence and who had no recourse to public funds. For those assessed as eligible, this support could be extended for up to 40 weeks (Eaves 2009). At the time of writing, this project had not been evaluated.

A useful Swedish study (Alizadeh et al 2010) describes the work of youth clinics run by midwives and counsellors in supporting young women at risk of 'honour' based violence. These clinics provide advice on sexual health and relationships and aim to promote gender equality. Focus groups with staff from five such clinics in Stockholm identified three key elements in their work; these are shown in Box 7.7.

Box 7.7: Key features of intervention with young women at risk of 'honour' based violence

1. Creating a safe place where young women can disclose their 'secret'.

2. Risk assessment that involves assessment of:

    > the young woman's own level of anxiety

    > the likelihood of disclosure of her 'secret'

    > the seriousness of the consequences of disclosure.

3. Worry-reducing measures which include:

    > empowerment – offering opportunities for thought and reflection in a supportive environment, providing advice on sexual health and a language for discussion of sexual health issues

    > keeping the secret – providing advice and treatment aimed at concealing loss of virginity

    > mediation – meetings with family members if disclosure was assessed as safe

    > secondary prevention in the form of advice about sexual health

(adapted from Alizadeh et al 2010, p36)

Youth clinic staff noted the tensions that existed between young women's wishes to free themselves of parental control while maintaining close ties with their families and workers commented that separation from their family was rarely the solution sought by young women using their service.

A study of the experiences of 30 women with disabilities who were domestic violence survivors (Hague et al 2008) found that some reported positive experiences of specialist domestic violence services, while the accessibility of refuges was a problem for others. Generally, refuges were only accessed by women with fewer support needs. When refuge staff made appropriate provision for disabled women the services were rated positively, but some women participating in this study complained of paternalistic attitudes from staff.

Counting the costs

A climate in which there is increasing pressure on services to demonstrate their cost-effectiveness has resulted in the development of evaluation approaches and tools that seek to calculate the health, welfare, social and economic costs of domestic violence in order to provide arguments for intervention; children's services costs are usually factored into these calculations. In the UK, this approach has been pioneered in the field of domestic violence by Stanko (Stanko et al 1998; Stanko 2001) and Walby (2004). While such approaches make for powerful arguments that can be used to unlock funding for interventions with families experiencing domestic violence, the calculations involved are inevitably imprecise and involve simplifying complex judgements that are open to challenge. For instance, Walby (2004) criticises Stanko et al's (1998) attribution of 22 per cent of the London Borough of Hackney's Child and Family costs to domestic violence on the grounds that, while 22 per cent of the borough's cases may have involved domestic violence, domestic violence on its own cannot account for all the service costs generated by child abuse and neglect. Walby (2004) allocates only half the costs of children's services' intervention in such families to domestic violence.

Walby (2004) developed this approach by using data from the Children in Need Census to calculate the total cost of children's social care services' expenditure on children in need for reasons of abuse and neglect in 2001 as £1.14 billion (this includes the costs of children who were looked after). She used evidence from a number of reviews and studies to conclude that domestic violence co-existed with child abuse in 40 per cent of these cases and took half this number of cases as 'a conservative estimate' of the proportion of children's services' workload that was 'driven by domestic violence' (Walby 2004), bringing the total estimated cost of domestic violence to children's services in one year to £22,869 million. She recalculated this figure for 2008 and found that a decrease in domestic violence, together with a small increase in the cost of public services, produced a new figure of £15,730 million (Walby 2009).

These approaches are still in the early stages of development; critics (Corso and Fertig 2010) of these models in child maltreatment note that they tend to be static – focused on a single cohort at a single point in time – rather than dynamic. Moreover, such models are only as good as the evidence that links experience of child harm to outcomes. These models require further refinement to close the gap between the complexity of the decisions informing cost allocation and the powerful simplicity of the final figures yielded by these methods.

Chapter seven: Summary

> This review found no evidence that parenting programmes are effective in reducing domestic violence.

> Early intervention programmes have been shown to be successful in reducing risks for victims and have also been used to deliver services to children. Families with more complex needs using these services have been found to require longer periods of intervention.

> Refuges provide a wide range of interventions for children but there has been little evaluation of this work. While the limited length of children's stay in a refuge may restrict opportunities for delivering interventions, a refuge stay may offer the opportunity for assessment and contact with relevant services in the community.

> Early evaluation of the Independent Domestic Violence Advisors service, which provides advocacy and service co-ordination for women experiencing domestic violence, suggests the service has been successful in reducing mothers' concerns about the harm their children experience from former partners. However, the service does not work directly with children.

> Safety planning is widely used in the UK but has not yet been evaluated in this context; however, US research has found that safety planning delivered in pregnancy increased women's use of safety measures.

> There is evidence from US and UK studies for the effectiveness of programmes that are delivered in parallel to children and their mothers. These interventions usually involve group work for children and groups for mothers that aim to develop responsiveness to the child's needs while offering support. Other interventions focus on providing support for mothers and children together in the aftermath of domestic violence. A key feature of all such interventions is the parent's engagement with the child's perspective on domestic violence.

> Psychotherapeutic and CBT treatments for parents and children have also been developed and studied in the US, but there is as yet little UK evidence available in relation to such interventions. Again, these programmes aim to develop mothers' appreciation of and responsiveness to the child's experience of domestic violence.

> Perpetrator programmes delivered in the US and the UK appear to be successful in reducing reoffending for the majority of participants and in improving victims' quality of life. Children's services are increasingly directing abusive men to attend voluntary perpetrator programmes as a means of protecting children. Early evaluation of local programmes in the UK suggests that such programmes have the potential to contribute to children's safety. Caring Dads is a programme recently introduced to the UK that focuses on the perpetrator's identity as a father. While there have been some positive reports from local evaluations, independent evaluations of this initiative were not available at the time of writing.

> There is evidence available for the effectiveness of interventions targeting domestic violence that focus on the whole family, although critics of such approaches have raised concern as to whether a whole-family approach can effectively contain men's power and control behaviours. A Canadian study found that a Family Group Decision Making approach was associated with reduced maltreatment of children. The early evaluation of Family Intervention Projects in England found that small caseloads, a key worker approach and long-term involvement all contributed to building a trusting relationship with families in which domestic violence could be addressed.

> Women with no recourse to public funds are particularly reliant on children's services' support to access a range of services for themselves and their children. They valued specialist services when these were made available to them.

> Similarly, women with disabilities found accessibility a problem in mainstream refuges and reported positive experiences of specialist services.

> This review identified increasing interest in developing methods for calculating the social and economic costs of domestic violence and such approaches usually include children's services' costs. While these approaches provide powerful arguments for introducing preventive interventions, at the time of writing they were still in their early stages of development.

Chapter eight

Interagency Collaboration

This chapter discusses the key challenges to effective interagency working in the context of domestic abuse, some examples of collaborative approaches to emerge from the literature and some recent developments of more integrated responses. Specifically, it includes consideration of the evidence relating to:

> identified challenges to collaboration, including limited information sharing between the police and child protection services, the need for robust information sharing protocols, and the need to ensure greater awareness and responsiveness to domestic violence among substance misuse and adult mental health services

> the use of particular strategies and approaches – such as interagency forums, integrated teams, co-location, secondment, joint protocols and link workers – to promote effective collaboration between agencies

> the effectiveness of Specialist Domestic Violence Courts

> interagency training.

A summary of key findings is set out at the end of the chapter.

The service response to domestic violence is acknowledged to be fragmented with a range of agencies conceptualising the issue differently, focusing on different actors within the family and offering very different interventions. While domestic violence constitutes a 'wicked' problem that requires a complex response which may only be partial (Devaney and Spratt 2009), the range of agencies involved and their varying approaches can be confusing and demanding for families, who may struggle first to disclose the problem and then to obtain appropriate support from services. Hester (2004) depicts the professional response to domestic violence as life on three separate planets; travel between these planets is often restricted. The three planets are shown in Figure 8.1: Planet A, the domestic violent planet, represents the position of criminal justice and specialist domestic violence agencies such as refuges; Planet B is the child protection sphere; and Planet C embodies private law intervention in the area of child contact. As Hester notes, while the criminal justice system takes a gendered approach, designating the man as perpetrator and the woman as victim, the other planets are more likely to take a non-gendered approach that emphasises parenting or shared custody and access. These different perspectives are described as leading to inconsistencies in practice that can jeopardise the safety of both mothers and children.

Figure 8.1: The Three Planets (Hester 2004, p1443)

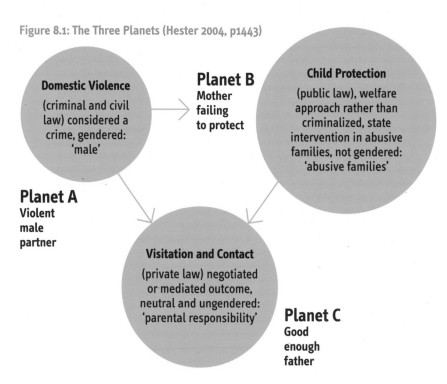

This galaxy could be extended further by adding in those spheres of professional activity focused on health, education and child development. These would include primary and secondary health-care services including child and adult mental health services, education and child psychology services, as well as a wide range of agencies focused on child welfare. While the police are often the first point of contact, domestic violence may be disclosed to practitioners in any of these services and an effective response in cases where children are experiencing harm is likely to involve the work of more than one agency. This chapter considers both the identified challenges for interagency communication and work, as well as examples of collaborative approaches described in the literature. Some recent developments of more integrated responses are also discussed. Where there is research or a local evaluation supporting initiatives these are cited but such evidence is not consistently available.

Challenges in interagency collaboration

In the first instance, interagency collaboration concerning families experiencing domestic violence needs to be informed by an awareness of safety issues in order that professional communication does not increase the likelihood of abuse and violence (Stanley and Humphreys 2006). Interagency protocols need to include guidelines on information transfer and confidentiality that agencies have signed up to and which are feasible for them to implement. The challenges involved in developing interagency responses are not located in any single agency. The interface between specialist domestic violence services and children's services provides a clear example of this. Stanley et al found that while many social workers were positive about the support specialist domestic violence workers offered families, others described them as 'very adult focused' (Stanley et al 2010c, p103). Analysis of assessments undertaken on 29 cases found no records of communication with specialist domestic violence services. Likewise, Cleaver et al's (2007) study of children's services' practice noted that these agencies were not involved in initial assessments or child protection case conferences.

While some aspects of this low level of collaboration may be attributed to social workers' attitudes and expectations of domestic violence agencies, the limited resources available to voluntary sector agencies may restrict their capacity to devote staff and time to interagency communication. Ball and Niven's (2007) Sure Start evaluation found that where representatives from specialist domestic violence agencies were included on Sure Start management committees, this acted to link Sure Start into the local multiagency structures for responding to domestic violence. However, some representatives from domestic violence agencies who had been involved in early partnership planning meetings ceased to attend when they could see no direct benefit for their agency.

The differing perspectives of children's services and the police were also identified by Stanley et al's (2010c) study. While social workers considered that police responses to victims of domestic violence had improved over time, they saw them as primarily adult-focused and more concerned with an immediate response than long-term intervention. This different timescale and focus on obtaining a criminal conviction was contrasted with the approach of children's services and was described as impacting on communication and collaboration.

> 'The police are focused on criminal proceedings; we are focused on child protection and safeguarding children ... The police have a role to play initially, and we have a role to play all the way through ... Sometimes it does feel that we are there to pick up the pieces ... other agencies can walk away, do their bit and walk away, we are there and we can be there for a long time. I think those type of issues do have an effect on, you know, on how each service perceives one another.'

> (A senior manager, children's services, quoted in Stanley et al 2010c, p193)

However, while Cross et al's (2005) research review also identified differences in attitudes, practice and perspectives between the police and child protection services, it highlighted the value of sharing information and concluded that joint work could convey authority and offer a means of managing safety concerns while promoting communication with families. Identified shortcomings in information exchange between the police and children's social care include insufficient (particularly in respect of children's experiences) and sometimes inaccurate information conveyed by the police, and a failure to consult with the police beyond the formal settings of child protection case conferences on the part of children's social care (Stanley et al 2010d).

Health professionals such as GPs, midwives, health visitors and accident and emergency staff are often the first professionals to receive disclosures of domestic violence both from victims and perpetrators (Lazenbatt and Greer 2009; Stanley et al 2009), but some studies have described a lack of awareness concerning domestic violence and its impact on children among them. Peckover's (2003) interviews with 24 health visitors found that their capacity to identify and name domestic violence varied considerably. However, Brooks et al's (2002) focus group study found that GPs and health visitors had a more fully developed understanding of domestic violence than other primary care professionals although, when considering the impact of domestic violence on children, both GPs and midwives refocused the discussion on adults. Hester (2006) reported that, when provided with appropriate tools and training, health visitors were able to develop their awareness and practice in relation to mothers' experiences of domestic violence.

Earlier chapters in this review identified mothers' mental health as a key factor mediating the impact of domestic violence on children. However, levels of awareness concerning the impact of domestic violence appear variable among practitioners in adult mental health services. Humphreys and Thiara's (2003) study of abused women's experiences of mental health services found that the responses of mental health professionals were characterised by a lack of acknowledgment of women's trauma, a failure to ask about domestic violence and victim blaming. A review of the research on domestic violence and severe psychiatric disorder (Howard et al 2009) found that adult mental health services only occasionally screened or used routine enquiry for domestic violence and that information about childhood and adult abuse rarely informed intervention.

Similarly, research with key informants in substance misuse services (Humphreys et al 2005) reported that different theoretical models and resource issues were identified as barriers to effective interagency communication between domestic violence and substance misuse agencies, as well as a lack of knowledge and training on domestic violence among substance misuse practitioners. Exploratory research with 13 informants from key substance misuse agencies (Galvani 2006) also found that practitioners in substance misuse services were described as rarely screening female service users for domestic violence and lacked the training that would assist them to do so and to respond adequately.

While there is evidence that child and adolescent mental health services (CAMHS) receive referrals and work with children experiencing domestic violence (Stanley et al 2010c), there is little published material available on CAMHS interventions with children experiencing domestic violence in England and Wales. The CAMHS mapping exercise for 2008-09 (Barnes et al 2010) reported that 320 of the services responding described themselves as providing targeted services for children experiencing domestic violence. The government's response (Department for Children, Schools and Families and Department of Health 2010) to the Independent Review of CAMHS identifies children experiencing domestic violence as a vulnerable group at whom services should be targeted. Moffitt and Caspi (1998) argue that the evidence concerning the relationship between children's exposure to domestic violence, the development of childhood conduct disorders and violence in young people's and adults' relationships, together with the association between domestic violence and child maltreatment, makes for a strong argument for mental health professionals to engage with domestic violence across the life cycle.

UK evidence concerning education professionals' interventions with children experiencing domestic violence is similarly scarce, although McGee's (2000) research identified that some schools and nurseries provided useful and sensitive support for both children and their mothers. This review has identified some small-scale studies (Byrne and Taylor 2007; Adamson and Deverell 2009) that have addressed education professionals' work in this area and a recent handbook (Sterne and Poole 2010) aimed at schools and early years settings suggests a growth of interest in domestic violence among those working in education. Further evaluation of the Common Assessment Framework in England and Wales may provide more evidence on how education professionals collaborate with other services in relation to children experiencing domestic violence.

A study of forced marriage in Luton (Khanum 2008) argues that schools need to be engaged in a co-ordinated response to this form of domestic violence, particularly when it involves child marriage. This case-study research concludes that teachers should be alert to the possibility that bullying and domestic violence in families may be an indication of plans for child marriage and that the forced marriage of an older sibling is a particularly strong risk factor that education staff should raise with other professionals, subject to the protection of an individual's confidentiality. A study of forced marriage (Kazimirski et al 2009) identified examples of schools using the Missing from Education provisions to engage with parents in families where forced marriage was threatened to convey disapproval of children missing school for extended periods and to emphasise the importance of completing education. However, this study acknowledged that prevention and interventions in relation to forced marriage could be constricted by fear of alienating community leaders and groups; such sensitivities need to be openly acknowledged and taken into account in interagency planning.

Promoting interagency collaboration

Statham's (2004) review of the evidence on the effectiveness of interventions for children living in 'special circumstances' (who include those experiencing domestic violence) identified three key factors contributing to success:

> a holistic, multiagency approach that addresses the needs of the whole child

> links between adults and children's services

> intensive targeted support within a framework of universal provision

(Statham 2004, p596).

The literature provides a number of descriptive examples of initiatives that embody one or more of these factors and which aim to create closer links between services through devices such as interagency forums, integrated teams, co-location or secondment schemes, shared protocols and procedures, link workers and joint training. However, only a few of these approaches have been systematically evaluated.

An early study of interagency domestic violence forums across the UK (Hague and Malos 1998) urged increased participation from social services departments while warning that specialist domestic violence agencies could become marginalised in these settings. This study, in common with more recent commentators (Potito et al 2009), highlighted the power differentials between different organisations involved in responding to domestic violence. A mapping study of statutory and voluntary agencies in the UK (Humphreys et al 2001) found that just under half the social services departments surveyed had domestic violence policies in place; many of these included guidelines for a local interagency strategy. The majority of participating social services departments had a representative attending the local domestic violence forum. Welsh's (2008) study undertaken between 1998 and 2001 compared three local interagency domestic violence partnerships in northern England. In common with Hague at al's (1996) research, she found that domestic violence organisations and the police continued to be the agencies with the highest levels of commitment to partnership meetings. The involvement of agencies such as health and social services was determined by the commitment of individual champions. Nevertheless, collaboration at a strategic level can bring a range of benefits for agencies. The Sure Start evaluation (Ball and Niven 2007) found that membership of the local domestic abuse forum or partnership could offer local programmes access to training, to police statistics on current local need and feedback from local survivors' group members.

The secondment or co-location of specialist domestic violence practitioners in children's social care and other settings has been used as a means of raising the awareness and capacity of the service response to domestic violence. Findlater and Kelly (1999) describe the location of domestic violence specialists in children's social services departments in Massachusetts and Oregon. Such staff may be employed directly by child protection services or bought in on a contract basis from specialist domestic violence services. Similar models are now in evidence in the UK: Part (2006) describes a joint initiative between the police and Barnardo's in Tayside, Scotland which located Barnardo's project workers alongside police officers. A survey and interviews with families using the service found mothers appreciated the flexibility of the Barnardo's service, which offered both support and counselling for survivors of domestic violence and individual sessions for children. The long-term nature of the Barnardo's intervention was also valued and this is consistent with evidence presented in the previous chapter that emphasised the need for sustained interventions with children and families.

A different form of collaboration involving the police and child mental health practitioners is embodied in the Child Development-Community Policing Program (CDCP) (Berkowitz and Marans 2000) established in Connecticut, US, in 1991. Supported by Yale University, the programme had the following elements:

> programme conferences – weekly meetings where officers, mental health practitioners and other professionals met to identify relevant interventions for children assessed as in need

> consultation service – child mental health practitioners provided an on-call consultation service which officers used for advice or to obtain immediate assessment and intervention with a family from a mental health practitioner

> joint child development seminars for police officers and newly qualified child mental health practitioners

> university fellowships for police officers who complete the seminar programme, supervise the work of other officers in relation to children exposed to domestic violence and accumulate relevant practice experience.

(Berkowitz and Marans 2000)

US programmes such as this often rely on the use of students undertaking qualifying training to deliver services. However, this may be preferable to the long waiting lists for CAMHS that can characterise families' experiences in England and Wales (Stanley et al 2010c). Berkowitz and Marans (2000) argue that the fast response offered by the CDCP service allowed clinicians to capture the child's experience of domestic violence more fully and achieve an understanding of the meaning that a particular incident has for the child at the time. They give the example of a 14-year-old boy who was distressed and traumatised by being mistakenly arrested at the scene of an incident and describe how speedy assessment and a co-ordinated response from the police and the clinician assisted recovery.

Casey et al (2007) describe the integrated response offered by the CDCP programme at a later date when the service was providing advocacy, which was delivered within five to seven days of the police attending an incident of domestic violence. Advocates were paired with police officers to facilitate communication and they offered safety planning and referral to relevant agencies, as well as psychological screening and crisis support. The researchers (Casey et al 2007) compared outcomes for 102 women receiving this service with those for 102 women where the police attended a domestic violence incident but there was no follow-up from the advocacy service. Twenty per cent of women who received the advocacy intervention were recorded by the police as having a repeat incident in the subsequent 12 months, compared to 42 per cent of the women in the comparison group, indicating the success of the intervention in reducing domestic violence incidents.

Coohey and Frazer (2006) provide an example of a service agreement between a domestic violence service and a children's mental health service in New South Wales, Australia. The service agreement focused on ensuring that domestic violence and its impact on children were identified, that interventions with families took place in the context of a safety plan and that continuity of care was prioritised.

Family Justice Centres

Family Justice Centres embody a 'one stop shop' response for victims of domestic violence that aims to address the fragmentation of services noted above. Staffed by multidisciplinary teams, they offer a range of services from one central location. These are likely to include legal and housing services, advice on finances, benefits and immigration issues, counselling and safety planning, facilities for medical examinations, adult education, substance misuse services and (in Newham) a forced marriage unit. It is not clear to what extent they provide services delivered directly to children. At the time of writing, they have been established in four sites in the UK — Berkshire, Croydon, Derby and Newham — using the model developed by Family Justice Centers in the US which originated in San Diego, California, and has now been replicated across the US and in Canada (www.familyjusticecenter.com/Details/San-Diego-Family-Justice-Center.html). Funding for UK centres is provided by local authorities and the police. While accounts of the work of the UK centres are available (Hocking 2007), this review could not locate any published independent evaluations of their work.

Interagency approaches to risk assessment and filtering

Extensive interagency collaboration is most likely to take place when there is a focus on risk. Radford et al (2006a) describe a joint working arrangement between the Domestic Violence Intervention Project (DVIP) and two London boroughs, which provided for DVIP staff to assess the risks posed to both victims and children by the perpetrator of domestic violence. Risk assessments were conducted at four different levels, which corresponded to the level of concern about the children and the family's degree of involvement with the child protection system. These risk assessments could be used to inform court proceedings if required; they included the perspectives of the perpetrator, victim and children and recommended treatment options. The service could also be utilised to measure change following an intervention.

Multi-Agency Risk Assessment Conferences (MARACs) have been introduced in England and Wales as a means of improving interagency collaboration and risk assessment in relation to high-risk victims of domestic violence. Robinson's (2004) evaluation of MARACs in Cardiff reported that they acted to increase information sharing and trust between agencies. While children are not the specific focus of MARAC risk assessments, Robinson found that the MARACs provided a setting where children's needs could be raised and discussed. MARACS also appear to be successful in preventing revictimisation: the evaluation reported that 6 in 10 women experienced no further threats or violence in the six months following the MARAC. Guidance is available that links the work of MARACs to that of Multi-Agency Public Protection Arrangements (MAPPAs) (National Offender Management Service, Public Protection Unit 2009).

Stanley et al's (2010d) research included a survey of LSCBs in England and Wales undertaken in 2007-08 to identify innovative approaches to the task of filtering police notifications of domestic violence incidents. Thirty brief accounts of local multiagency initiatives were received from Chairs of LSCBs or their nominated respondent. It was notable that the agencies most frequently described as contributing to these initiatives were children's services and the police; health and education services were cited as participating partners in about half the approaches reported. Specialist domestic violence services in the voluntary sector were involved in just under half these initiatives. There was even less involvement from services for perpetrators: the probation service was described as a partner in just eight areas, and there was no involvement reported from voluntary sector services for perpetrators. CAMHS, adult mental health services and housing were only involved in one or two of the initiatives reported.

The study identified three key approaches to interagency assessment of risk that also sought to manage the volume of notifications:

A. interagency panels, integrated teams or co-located staff

B. police risk assessments utilised to route notifications

C. early intervention initiatives.

A. Interagency panels/integrated teams/co-locations: A third of the responses received described the establishment of regular interagency panels, integrated teams or co-location schemes that assessed risks for children and filtered notifications. Some areas had located social workers in police stations or established an integrated domestic violence team that undertook these tasks. Such arrangements appeared to have the benefit of allowing children's services direct access to police records so increasing the amount of information available to inform the assessment. Thiara and Chung (2008) evaluated the Domestic Violence and Abuse Notifications Screening Pilot in Coventry involving a half-time senior social worker, a children's services clerical officer and two full-time equivalent specialist police officers. This initiative resulted in a reduction in re-referrals to children's services. The evaluation identified a need for preventative work to be undertaken with those cases not receiving a service from children's social work services and Barnardo's became involved with a view to taking on some of this work. The evaluation noted the need for risk assessment and screening tools to be developed further and emphasised the need for sufficient allocation of staff time to the project.

B. Police risk assessments utilised to route notifications: Stanley et al (2010d) identified examples of systems whereby the police filtered and routed notifications directly to services according to established protocols or risk-assessment procedures. The Blackpool Domestic Abuse Team, whose work is described in Box 8.1, uses a variant on this approach. Such approaches in effect allow the police to filter notifications on behalf of children's services. However, as Humphreys (2007) has noted, police risk-assessment tools rely on a checklist approach rather than a dialogue with victims, who arguably possess the fullest information pertaining to risks. Moreover, Stanley et al's (2010c) study found that the police did not have a close focus on children involved in domestic violence incidents; in fact, there was limited evidence of police officers talking to children.

Some areas had developed a combination of approaches A and B, as the example below in Box 8.1 demonstrates. The Children's IDVA Service is an innovative but as yet unevaluated aspect of this service; in Scotland, the Caledonian System, which delivers programmes for convicted perpetrators of domestic violence crimes, also provides a service for children in addition to support for perpetrators' partners (The Scottish Government 2010).

> **Box 8.1: Blackpool Domestic Abuse Team**
>
> The multiagency Blackpool Domestic Abuse Team is funded by Blackpool Council, Lancashire Police and the local NHS. The unit is responsible for orchestrating the work of over 40 agencies across the town and for organising MARACs, in addition to delivering the Sanctuary Service and work in schools. The Domestic Abuse Team has commissioned the Children's IDVA Service (a Home Office pilot introduced in 2009), which supports children and young people aged up to 21 affected by domestic violence. The Children's IDVA Service accepts referrals from a number of sources, including self-referrals from young people, and has worked with over 300 children in its first two years.
>
> The Catalyst Team was introduced in July 2009 and includes specialist police officers and children's services social workers co-located in a police station. The team is responsible for screening notifications and undertaking initial assessments in a timely manner in conjunction with police officers, health workers and IDVAs.
>
> The Catalyst Team assign a risk level using the ACPO DASH (Richards et al 2008) risk assessment model. Low-risk incidents are sent to children's social care services, specialist domestic violence agencies, the NHS and Pupil Welfare (who forward the case to the relevant school). At a medium level of risk, incidents are sent to these same organisations but are allocated priority. High-risk incidents are additionally routed to the Adults and Children's IDVA services and automatically referred on to the MARAC.
>
> There is some indication to date that co-location has enabled early intervention with families but no formal evaluation of the service or the teams has been completed.

C. Early intervention initiatives: Stanley et al's (2010c) survey found a range of examples where the police provided victims with information about specialist domestic violence services and, if the victim gave consent, made a referral to that agency on their behalf. In Brighton and Hove, specialist domestic violence services were automatically informed of all incidents by the police and letters were sent from this service to victims. In this area, perpetrators could also be offered a referral to a local voluntary sector service for perpetrators. However, Part's (2006) account of the Tayside scheme discussed above appears to be one of the few published UK examples of police routing families to a service that specifically targets children exposed to domestic violence.

The Green Book – enhancing collaboration

The Greenbook guidance, Effective Intervention in Domestic Violence and Child Maltreatment Cases: Guideline for policy and practice (National Council of Juvenile and Family Court Judges) was produced in the US in 1999. It includes a set of principles for ensuring the safety and well-being of all victims of domestic violence and recommends active collaboration and co-ordination of the work of agencies involved in domestic violence and child protection. A five-year programme to implement the guidance ran from 2000 to 2005 in six sites in five US states (Edleson and Malik 2008). Led by the judiciary, the initiative focused on the child welfare system, specialist domestic violence services and the courts. The key features of the project and the evaluation findings are shown in Box 8.2.

Box 8.2: The Greenbook Initiative

How the Greenbook was implemented:

> Representation from staff at multiple levels from the full range of organisations at interagency forums and meetings

> Survivor representation on interagency forums (although this involvement decreased over time)

> Screening and assessment protocols

> Multiagency teams, groups and responses – reviewed, filtered and routed cases

> Co-located and specialist staff located in range of agencies

> Training focused on understanding the dynamics of interagency work

Factors facilitating collaboration:

> 'Institutional empathy' – understanding of the context shaping how another agency works

> Effective and neutral leaders – who had a broad vision of what system change would look like and understood different perspectives

> Reaching out to the community – involved disseminating awareness and building support beyond collaboration partners

> Needs analyses – logic models used to link needs with objectives

> Frontline multiagency approaches were rated as most effective by stakeholders:

  > specialist/co-located posts helped shift agency practice

  > multiagency teams/review meetings reduced mother-blaming, provided support and advocacy for all family members and co-ordinated interventions.

(Banks et al 2008a)

Specialist Domestic Violence Courts – forging links across services

Specialist Domestic Violence Courts have been operating in the UK since 1999 when the first such court was established in Leeds. The Domestic Violence Crime and Victims Act 2004 made provision for the establishment of a series of courts in other UK cities that drew on models from the US where domestic violence courts first emerged in the early 1980s (Eley 2005; Hester et al 2008). Such courts are specialist criminal courts at magistrates' level that deal with all domestic violence cases so they can be speedily managed by court officers and other professionals with specialist training and relevant experience. They aim to enhance victim safety but also have the capacity to offer a more co-ordinated response to domestic violence by bringing together both civil and criminal cases and by establishing fast-track routes into perpetrator programmes (Eley 2005). Eley's (2005) evaluation of the work of such a court in Toronto found that victims were provided with support and that the number of offenders directed to treatment programmes increased. She argues that the success of domestic violence courts rests in their process, which has their capacity to achieve co-ordination and collaboration between the different actors and organisations involved in responding to domestic violence.

An evaluation of the first five Specialist Domestic Violence Courts in England and Wales (Welsh 2008) found that multiagency partnership approaches were a crucial element in their success. Support services for victims were judged effective, the courts had facilitated the delivery of advocacy and information services and victims' participation and satisfaction was improved. However, child protection awareness and initiatives were found to vary across the sites and the researchers recommended that the courts needed to take account of family and civil proceedings in relation to children, suggesting this as an area for future development (Cook et al 2004). In the light of this, an evaluation (Hester et al 2008) of the Integrated Domestic Violence Court in Croydon proved disappointing. The Croydon court was established as a pilot with the specific aim of integrating criminal proceeding with family proceedings (both Children's Act and civil injunction proceedings). In its first year, only five cases proceeded through the court although approximately 75 had been anticipated; the domestic violence advocacy service, which was to have provided support to victims, appeared to disengage from the work of the court and the multiagency management group lost most of its members from agencies outside criminal justice (Hester et al 2008). The small number of victims who participated in the evaluation considered that the court had not shown an appreciation of the impact of domestic violence on children and that its work had been dominated by a presumption of contact.

Innovative approaches to child contact and domestic violence

Brown (2006) describes two Australian models for integrated court systems that address allegations of child abuse that arise in the context of disputes about child custody and contact. The Magellan programme, which was introduced nationally in 2003, involves a multidisciplinary court team and takes an interagency approach. The formal evaluation found that co-operation between the court and child protection services improved substantially with all families being investigated, reports being completed more quickly and allegations of abuse more likely to be substantiated. The average number of court events and length of the process also fell. Final orders were more likely to involve supervised contact or no contact and, at 12-month follow-up, final orders were also less likely to have broken down (Brown 2006).

The Columbus programme is a similar approach introduced in Western Australia that also involves a multidisciplinary court team: a child protection officer is present for all family court hearings addressing custody or access issues. It differs from the Magellan programme in its definition of exposure to domestic violence as a form of child abuse but has not been evaluated to date (Brown 2010).

In New Zealand, the Guardianship Act was amended in 1995 following the deaths of three children whose father had been given interim custody of them despite protection orders having been made as a consequence of his violence towards their mother (Busch and Robertson 2000). The family court now operates on the presumption that a parent who has used violence against a child or against the other parent will not be awarded custody or unsupervised access unless the court is satisfied of the child's safety during contact. Busch and Robertson's (2000) review of the impact of this legislative change found that gaps between the law and its implementation remained. They note the need for protection orders for victims to be enforced, for women and children to have access to the financial and housing resources that allow them to live independently of the perpetrator and for secure supervised access centres to permit safe access (see also Chapter 7).

Training and supervision

Banks et al (2008b) report that at the outset of the Greenbook project, training for child welfare social workers tended to be optional, to address only basic issues and to be hampered by high turnover in the workforce. Interagency training delivered as part of this initiative addressed staff's understanding of other agencies' systems and of confidentiality and the other constraints on interagency collaboration. The evaluation (Banks et al 2008b) found that training initiatives, together with co-located advocates and other work on developing relationships with specialist domestic violence agencies, led to increased awareness of domestic violence among child welfare workers, collaborative work and sharing of resources and expertise. The researchers emphasise the need for new policies and protocols to be consistently reinforced by training.

In common with these findings, Stanley et al (2010d) found that both police and social workers participating in their UK study emphasised a need for training that would enhance their understanding of one another's roles. It was argued that knowing more about the agency that information was being sent to would improve the quality of information transfer:

> '... we need to be having joint training and things like that to improve it, to know each other's parts, what we do, because I still don't know what other agencies do properly, I know they do something but I don't know what.'
>
> (Domestic violence specialist police officer, quoted in Stanley et al 2010d, p12)

One study found that over a third of 33 managers from children's social care, police, health and housing rated their knowledge of domestic violence as adequate or poor (Cleaver et al 2007). Levels of knowledge and confidence were found to reflect the amount of training delivered in an area. The researchers argue that training should be given higher priority. Their survey of managers and trainers identified four factors that supported the delivery of training:

> ensuring sufficient time and resources are available for staff to participate

> providing multiagency training that linked initiatives

> targeting training on staff from 'hard to engage' organisations

> auditing and monitoring training.

(Cleaver et al 2007)

Various other services identify a need for specific training on domestic violence. Brooks and Webb (2007) suggest that CAMHS professionals would benefit from training in this area.

Hendry (1998) outlined three key aims for training programmes on domestic violence:

1. Training should be informed by research evidence and practice experience.

2. It should raise awareness of the nature and impact of domestic violence and its relationship with other forms of child harm:

> If training achieves anything, it must ensure that when we become aware of domestic violence we explore the possibility of harm to any children, and that conversely when we become aware of child protection concerns, we explore the possibility that domestic violence is taking place.
>
> (Hendry 1998, p131)

3. It should provide practitioners with the skills and knowledge to ask direct questions about domestic violence, to assess needs and risk and provide accurate advice and information.

She also identified five key questions for developing a training strategy on domestic violence. These are shown in Box 8.3.

Box 8.3: Key questions to inform a training strategy on domestic violence

1. Who should be trained with who – ie which agencies should be involved, should there be opportunities for single gender training?

2. What different levels of training are required – eg awareness raising, specialist?

3. How can training programmes be delivered to maximize access and to be cost-effective?

4. What adaptations are needed to existing programmes to ensure that domestic violence is addressed?

5. How will the impact of programmes and the strategy as a whole be addressed?

(Hendry 1998, p132-133)

Chapter eight: Summary

> The service response to domestic violence is fragmented; this creates barriers to disclosure and accessing support for families, as well as limiting information transfer between agencies, and so reduces the amount of information available to inform assessments.

> Children's social care services could usefully increase ongoing communication with both specialist domestic violence services and the police, rather than confining it to formal settings such as case conferences.

> There is evidence that primary health-care professionals who receive appropriate training have raised levels of awareness regarding domestic violence but the awareness of practitioners in adult mental health and substance misuse services, who frequently encounter both perpetrators and victims of domestic violence in their practice, appears less well developed. These groups of professionals might benefit from involvement in interagency training initiatives.

> While CAMHS professionals are known to work with children and families experiencing domestic violence, there is little evidence available about the nature of their work in this field. Further research is needed in this area and collaboration with children's services might be improved by involving CAMHS staff in relevant training.

> Improved interagency collaboration has been achieved when the full range of organisations is represented by staff from all levels – but particularly senior levels – at interagency forums and meetings, and when shared protocols for screening and assessment are introduced.

> Co-location, interagency meetings and integrated teams can provide an effective means by which agencies can share information as part of the processes of both filtering referrals and assessing risk.

> Co-location and secondment schemes involving different agencies have aimed at ensuring families receive early intervention. Family Justice Centres provide an example of a highly integrated service for victims of domestic violence, but these have not yet been independently evaluated in the UK.

> In England and Wales, specialist Domestic Violence Courts have been successful in increasing sensitivity to and support for victims of domestic violence and engaging perpetrators in treatment. However, a pilot project that aimed to co-ordinate the work of such a court with that of family proceedings courts was less successful. Australia provides examples of courts that take an integrated approach to child contact and child protection. New Zealand law includes a presumption of 'no contact' in cases where a parent has used domestic violence.

> Interagency training should aim to ensure that practitioners develop an appreciation of the perspectives of other agencies in addition to raising awareness of the nature and impact of domestic violence and its impact on children.

Chapter nine

Conclusion

This chapter provides a brief summary of the key themes and patterns of effective service delivery to emerge from this review of the research. It offers an overview of messages addressing:

> prevention and early intervention

> managing the volume of work

> engaging and intervening with families, including:

>> work with violent fathers

>> mothers' and children's mental health

>> views of children and young people

>> work with adolescents

>> the role of refuge services

> and the importance of interagency work.

The chapter concludes by identifying the main features and key steps towards developing a responsive service.

This review has emphasised that domestic violence is a sustained process rather than a single event. It occurs in the context of other forms of disadvantage and interacts with these different sources of stress and with other family problems associated with domestic violence to harm children's health and well-being. This harm manifests itself in varying ways at different stages in children's development.

Children's experience of domestic violence is a complex problem because the harm is cumulative. Holt et al's (2008) research review of the impact of exposure to domestic violence on children concludes by emphasising that there is rarely a straightforward causal pathway leading to specific outcomes. For example, domestic violence damages mothers' self-esteem and mental health, and so compromises their parenting and their capacity to protect children from the fear and worry evoked by exposure to domestic violence. Furthermore, ongoing domestic violence isolates mothers and children from their local communities, both while it is happening and once families have separated. This isolation may reduce the sources of support for children and young people – for instance, they may lose friendships and relationships that contribute to resilience. Children's experience of domestic violence can also co-exist with other forms of child abuse and neglect in the family.

This picture of cumulative harm means that intervention needs to take place at a number of levels and to address a range of issues. The knowledge to inform effective information will therefore come from a range of fields. This review has aimed to bring this body of information together and interrogate it to answer some key questions relevant for those planning and delivering services. In doing so, several major gaps in knowledge have emerged. Some of these gaps, such as the lack of evidence on the parenting of violent fathers and the limited knowledge concerning the effectiveness of safety planning and interventions for children delivered in refuges, are characteristic of the international literature. Other shortfalls in the evidence base are specific to the UK; these include the lack of knowledge concerning the work of children's mental health services in this field and the small number of independent evaluations of interventions for children experiencing domestic violence.

However, this review has demonstrated that there is now a substantial if uneven body of knowledge available to inform the work of practitioners, managers and planners. Practitioners' awareness of and commitment to working to reduce the effects of domestic violence on children has increased substantially in the last decade and it is possible to be hopeful that the key messages generated by this review will evoke interest and be used to inform policy and practice; these messages are listed below.

Prevention

Preventive programmes delivered in school settings have had some success in raising awareness and knowledge of relevant sources of help and in changing children and young people's attitudes. Not enough is known about the optimum timing, frequency and content for these programmes, but locating them within the school curriculum is likely to make for more regular delivery. Such programmes need to take account of gender and they could usefully target boys' low awareness of the harmful effects of abusive behaviour.

Awareness of domestic violence in the wider community has increased as a result of a range of community education programmes but attitudes and behaviour may be resistant to change in some communities where traditional conceptions of gender roles and patriarchy have been slow to shift. Targeting campaigns on the attitudes and behaviours of particular groups such as male perpetrators may be the most effective approach at this point in time (see Stanley et al 2009).

Early interventions

Pregnancy involves increased risk of domestic violence for a substantial minority of women. It is also a time when women will have increased contact with health services and motivation for change may be high. Pregnancy therefore offers a useful site for early interventions such as screening and advocacy services.

Early evaluation of UK Independent Domestic Violence Advisors (IDVA) services for women experiencing domestic violence has shown some positive short-term outcomes. However, these services do not as yet include a direct focus on children. Early intervention projects that include direct work with children have produced positive results (Donovan et al 2010), but such services need to ensure that robust multiagency partnerships are established in the developmental phase of these initiatives.

Managing the volume of work with children and families experiencing domestic violence

The high volume of notifications of children experiencing domestic violence represents a major challenge for children's social care. The current system is inefficient and ineffective, with many families rotating through children's social care but not receiving sustained interventions. The evidence indicates that not all children will be harmed by exposure to domestic violence, but systems for identifying those who will and won't need a service are still embryonic.

Notifications need to be filtered, a process that involves assessing the risks for children. Co-location schemes or integrated teams allow information from multiple sources to be shared and to inform this process of risk assessment. If police officers' assessments are to be used to route notifications, their assessments will need to be more child-focused and they will need to engage more fully with children and young people at domestic violence incidents.

Letters sent to families by children's social care services in the absence of any other intervention appear ineffective in reducing either domestic violence or the demands on services and may increase the risk of violence.

Engaging with families experiencing domestic violence

The stigma and secrecy associated with domestic violence, together with the potential for state intervention to provoke further abuse and the threat of children being removed from families, make it likely that children's social care interventions will be resisted by families experiencing domestic violence. Threatening mothers experiencing domestic violence with statutory intervention if they fail to protect children will have the effect of increasing distrust and is likely to be ineffective if the abuse originates with her partner or if the couple have already separated.

Children's social care practitioners should seek to build partnerships with families based on a shared understanding of the impact of domestic violence on children and young people. Enabling both parents to recognise and engage with the child's experience of domestic violence can offer a means of building motivation for change in both mothers and fathers. This requires practitioners to work with both parents, but not necessarily together.

Sustained deep interventions

Intervention with families where children are experiencing harm as a consequence of domestic violence needs to be sufficiently deep and sustained to build the trust and confidence that enable families to disclose domestic violence and practitioners to engage with children, mothers and fathers, and to develop the motivation and confidence to change behaviour.

Practitioners may be too ready to associate separation with safety: domestic violence often continues beyond the point of separation, and separated women and women on their own with children are those most likely to be victims of domestic violence. Contact with children also offers a context in which children continue to experience domestic violence. Establishing separation as the primary goal of intervention can result in a stop-start approach to intervention where large numbers of large families are recycled through children's social care referral and assessment systems.

While there is evidence that practitioners from the same community as their clients can offer culturally sensitive interventions and foster trust, BME women and young people have also expressed concerns about confidentiality when disclosing domestic violence to members of their own community.

Violent fathers

The limited research evidence concerning fathering by violent men mirrors the lack of a focus on them in practice. A failure to engage with fathers in families where children experience domestic violence leaves mothers who are themselves victims carrying the responsibility for managing men's violence. A shortfall in information concerning perpetrators, together with the restricted time frame for initial assessment, contributes to the exclusion of fathers from practice and this exclusion compounds the lack of information (Baynes and Holland 2010). When it is available, social workers find information concerning violent fathers' criminal histories valuable and this should be consistently accessed from the police and fed into assessments.

There is evidence for the effectiveness of perpetrator programmes. Children's social care in England and Wales is increasingly identifying voluntary perpetrator programmes as a resource for intervening with abusive fathers; however, currently these programmes are sparsely distributed. Where social workers direct fathers to these programmes, men's participation may initially be motivated by the prospect of obtaining access to children or avoiding care proceedings. However, these instrumental attitudes do not appear to act as barriers to the success of the programmes in changing abusive behaviour.

Since these programmes are currently few in number, children's social care cannot wholly delegate the task of intervening to change abusive behaviour to them. Staff delivering such programmes will have accumulated a wealth of knowledge and skills in working with violent fathers that social workers could access through training. Children's social care practitioners need to build their skills and confidence in work with violent fathers. Furthermore, the restrictions on the time frame for initial assessments need to be relaxed in order to allow social workers to engage with fathers.

Mothers' and children's mental health

Domestic violence compromises mothers' mental health; and mental health problems, together with the direct effects of domestic violence, undermine parenting. Interventions that address mothers' mental health as well as promoting their relationships with their children and securing their safety are therefore valuable.

Practitioners in adult mental health services may need training to raise their awareness of the impact of domestic violence and to promote interagency communication and collaboration in cases of domestic violence. Screening for domestic violence could be introduced in adult mental health services, as this has proved effective in other health settings when accompanied by relevant training for staff.

While child and adolescent mental health services (CAMHS) are known to undertake work in relation to domestic violence, this review encountered few accounts of this work in the UK context. More needs to be known about CAMHS interventions in this area. There are innovative examples from other countries of joint initiatives between a range of agencies and children's mental health services that could be emulated.

Listening to children and young people

Although children and young people's involvement in domestic violence is intimate and active, they report that they are often excluded from professional interventions. Fears that they will not be listened to, and that their experience and views will not be taken seriously or treated confidentially, act as barriers to disclosure of domestic violence and help-seeking. This applies both to children living with domestic violence in their parents' relationship and for young people experiencing violence in their own intimate relationships. This latter group require social workers to focus on them and their relationships with their peers, as well as seeing them as part of their family.

Practitioners need to elicit and respect children's views on contact, to distinguish between safe and unsafe contact and to identify means of ensuring contact is safe.

Working with adolescents

This review found that domestic violence can feature in the lives of adolescents in two key ways: as a feature of their parents' relationships and in their own relationships. Those who experience the first of these forms of abuse are more likely to experience the second. Practitioners should consistently ask young people about their experiences of domestic violence in their own and their parents' relationships, particularly when young people have mental health problems or when they are looked after/care leavers or young parents.

Young people seem to value in particular the support they receive in their relationships from practitioners, such as mentors or staff at youth clinics in Sweden, whose role outside mainstream provision may allow them to be perceived as more accessible and trustworthy than teachers or social workers.

Interventions for mothers and children

Interventions for mothers and children together build on the knowledge that resilience is fostered by a supportive relationship with a caring adult. These interventions should be directed towards strengthening that bond as well as to developing children and young people's self-esteem and reducing their self-blame. Models for such services are available from North America and Australia and some services that focus on mothers and children, or on the whole family, are emerging in England and Wales.

There is evidence that mothers' parenting can recover from the effects of domestic violence, although generic parenting programmes such as the Family Nurse Partnership seem less effective with families experiencing domestic violence.

A key feature of those mother-child interventions that have been positively evaluated is an emphasis on enabling the parent to engage with and increase their responsiveness to the child's perspective on domestic violence.

Refuge services for children

Refuges in England and Wales are delivering a range of interventions for children and young people but not enough is known about these. A stay in a refuge offers an opportunity for children and young people's needs to be assessed and for them to be linked into mainstream health and social care services. More might be made of this opportunity. Additionally, mothers and children need to be connected with community support systems when they leave the refuge, as this is described as a difficult and potentially isolating time for them. This may be particularly the case for BME families and for families where mothers or children are disabled.

Interagency work

Children's experience of domestic violence is associated with a range of other parental problems including substance misuse, homelessness and learning difficulties, as well as parental mental health problems. This requires children's social care to work closely with a range of other agencies; communication with the police and specialist domestic violence agencies needs to be ongoing rather than confined to child protection meetings.

At the time of writing, there is limited evidence on the role of the Common Assessment Framework in facilitating interagency work on domestic violence. Research in this area should include a focus on schools as little is known about their work with children experiencing domestic violence.

Specialist domestic violence courts that bring together a range of agencies to ensure the delivery of advocacy and information for victims have proved successful in the UK but progress towards integrating such courts with family proceedings has been slow.

Both co-location schemes and interagency training that addresses the different contexts and perspectives agencies bring to domestic violence work have been found to be effective in promoting collaboration.

Developing new approaches in children's social care

This review has identified some key features of a service that is responsive to the needs of children experiencing domestic violence.

A responsive service is one which:

> engages with families on the basis of shared perceptions of harm experienced by children living with domestic violence, rather than utilising blame and threats

> seeks to involve all family members, including perpetrators, while recognising that it may not always be safe or appropriate to see all family members together

> distinguishes appropriate pathways for families experiencing domestic violence using risk assessment that incorporates evidence from the full range of services

> recognises the need for long-term engagement with families with complex needs and embedded histories of domestic violence that is not predicated on separation.

Box 9.1 - overleaf - shows key steps towards developing a responsive service that have emerged from this review.

Box 9.1: Key steps towards developing a responsive service

Commissioning

> Early intervention services require the support of senior managers from the full range of services in order to be able to link families to these services effectively.

> Voluntary programmes for perpetrators that address their role as fathers can help reduce men's violence and increase their awareness of its impact on children.

> Parallel interventions for both mothers and children that develop mothers' understanding and responsiveness to children's experience of domestic violence, while strengthening children's self-esteem, offer a means of building resilience and promoting recovery.

Developing interagency collaboration

> Mechanisms should be identified for increasing ongoing communication with both specialist domestic violence services and the police.

> Co-location schemes that allow children's social care and other agencies such as the police to share the information required to assess risk should be developed.

> Children's social care should collaborate with adult mental health services and CAMHS to increase their sensitivity to domestic violence and its impact on children and to develop therapeutic interventions for mothers and children.

> Systems for collaboration need to be developed with practitioners in an 'intermediate' position – such as school mentors – who offer a means of intervening with young people experiencing violence in their relationships.

> Closer collaboration with refuges should aim to incorporate the work they undertake with children into wider assessments of children's needs.

Strengthening practice

> Practitioners need to be skilled in talking directly to children about domestic violence and listening to and validating their accounts.

> Work with adolescents, particularly looked after children and care leavers, should address their peer relationships; they should be routinely asked about their experiences of domestic violence in their own and their parents' relationships.

> Training in work with violent men should be made available to practitioners and their managers.

> Interagency training that addresses variations in agency approaches and objectives in work with families experiencing domestic violence can strengthen collaboration.

References

Abrahams H (2007) *Supporting Women after Domestic Violence: Loss, trauma and recovery.* London: Jessica Kingsley Publishers

Adamson S and Deverell C (2009) 'CAF in the Country: Implementing the Common Assessment Framework in a rural area' *Child and Family Social Work* 14 (4) 400-409

ADVA (Against Domestic Violence and Abuse In Devon) and Sue Penna Associates (2009) *REPAIR (Resolve to End the Perpetration of Abuse in Relationships): A Community and Whole family based Intervention Programme Targeting Perpetrators of Domestic Violence and Abuse in Devon. An evaluation of a three year Invest to Save (ISB) Project.* Exeter: Devon County Council

Afzal N (2009) 'Prosecuting Violence Against Women.' (Paper presented at BASPCAN Conference, *New Challenges in Protecting Women and Children,* 11 December 2009.) London: Institute of Child Health

Alexander H, Macdonald E and Paton S (2005) 'Raising the Issue of Domestic Abuse in Schools' *Children and Society* 19 (3) 187-198

Alizadeh V, Hylander I, Kocturk T and Tornkvist L (2010) 'Counselling Young Immigrant Women Worried about Problems Related to the Protection of "Family Honour" – From the perspective of midwives and counsellors at youth health clinics' *Scandinavian Journal of Caring Sciences* 24 (1) 32-40

Almedia RV and Dolan-Delvecchio K (1999) 'Addressing Culture in Batterers Intervention: The Asian Indian community as an illustrative example' *Violence Against Women* 5 (6) 654-683

Anitha S (2010) 'No Recourse, No Support: State policy and practice towards South Asian women facing domestic violence in the UK' *British Journal of Social Work* 40 (2) 462-479

Anooshian L (2005) 'Violence and Aggression in the Lives of Homeless Children: A review' *Aggression and Violent Behavior* 10 (2) 129-152

Antle B, Barbee A, Sullivan D, Yankeelov P, Johnson L and Cunningham M (2007) 'The Relationship between Domestic Violence and Child Neglect' *Brief Treatment and Crisis Intervention* 7 (4) 364-382

Appel AE and Holden GW (1998) 'The Co-occurrence of Spouse and Physical Child Abuse: A review and appraisal' *Journal of Family Psychology* 12 (4) 578-599

Australian Institute of Health and Welfare (2005) 'Female SAAP Clients and Children Escaping Domestic and Family Violence 2003–04' *AIHW Bulletin* 30 (September)

Avery-Leaf S, Cascardi DM, O'Leary D and Cano A (1997) 'Efficacy of a Dating Violence Prevention Program on Attitudes Justifying Aggression' *Journal of Adolescent Health* 21 (1) 11-17

Bacchus L, Mezey G, Bewley S and Haworth S (2004) 'Prevalence of Domestic Violence when Midwives Routinely Enquire in Pregnancy' *BJOG: An International Journal of Obstetrics and Gynaecology* 111 (5) 441-445

Baldry E, Bratel J and Breckenridge J (2006) 'Domestic Violence and Children with Disabilities: Working towards enhancing social work practice' *Australian Social Work* 59 (2) 185-197

Ball M and Niven L (2007) *Sure Start Local Programmes and Domestic Abuse.* Nottingham: HMSO

Bancroft L and Silverman JG (2002) *The Batterer as Parent: Addressing the impact of domestic violence on family dynamics.* New York: Sage

Banister E and Leadbeater BJ (2007) 'To Stay or to Leave? How do mentoring groups support healthy dating relationships in high-risk girls?' in Leadbeater B and Way N (eds), *Urban Girls Revisited: Building strengths.* New York: New York University Press

Banks D, Dutch N and Wang K (2008a) 'Collaborative Efforts to Improve System Response to Families who are Experiencing Child Maltreatment and Domestic Violence' *Journal of Interpersonal Violence* 23 (7) 876-902

Banks D, Landsverk J and Wang K (2008b) 'Changing Policy and Practice in the Child Welfare System through Collaborative Efforts to Identify and Respond Effectively to Family Violence' *Journal of Interpersonal Violence* 23 (7) 903-932

Barnard M (2007) *Drug Addiction and Families.* London: Jessica Kingsley Publishers

Barnes D, Devanney C, Uglebjerg A, Wistow R and Hartley C (2010) *A Profile of Children's Health, Child and Adolescent Mental Health Services and Maternity Services in England* 2008/9. Durham: School of Applied Social Sciences, University of Durham

Barnes J, Ball M, Meadows P, Belsky J and the FNP Implementation Research Team (2009) *Nurse-Family Partnership Programme. Second Year Pilot Sites Implementation in England: The infancy period.* (Research Report No DCSF-RR166.) London: Department for Children, Schools and Families

Barron J (2007) *Kidspeak – Giving children and young people a voice on domestic violence.* Bristol: Women's Aid Federation of England. Available online at www. womensaid.org.uk/core/core_picker/download.asp?id=1498 (Accessed 14 October 2010)

Barter C (2009) 'In the Name of Love: Partner abuse and violence in teenage relationships' *British Journal of Social Work* 39 (2) 211-233

Barter C, McCarry M, Berridge D and Evans K (2009) *Partner Exploitation and Violence in Teenage Intimate Relationships.* London: NSPCC / Bristol: University of Bristol School of Policy Studies. Available online at www.nspcc.org.uk/Inform/research/ findings/partner_exploitation_and_violence_report_wdf70129.pdf (Accessed 16 October 2010)

Barth RP (2009) 'Preventing Child Abuse and Neglect with Parent Training: Evidence and opportunities' *Future of Children* 19 (2) 95-118

Baynes P and Holland S (2010) 'Social Work with Violent Men: A child protection file study in an English local authority' *Child Abuse Review* Early view: doi: 10.1002/ car.1159 http://onlinelibrary.wiley.com/doi/10.1002/car.1159/abstract (Accessed 20 December 2010)

Becker F and French L (2004) 'Making the Links: Child abuse, animal cruelty and domestic violence' *Child Abuse Review* 13 (6) 399-414

Becker F and French L (2006) 'Response to "Forging the Links: (De)constructing chains of behaviours"' *Child Abuse Review* 15 (3) 188-189

Becker S, Aldridge J and Dearden C (1998) *Young Carers and their Families.* Oxford: Blackwell

Bell J and Stanley N (2005) *Tackling Domestic Violence at the Local Level: An evaluation of the Preston Road Domestic Violence Project.* Hull: University of Hull

Bell J and Stanley N (2006) 'Learning about Domestic Violence: Young people's responses to a Healthy Relationships Programme' *Sex Education* 6 (3) 237-250

Bell M and McGoren J (2003) *Domestic Violence Risk Assessment Model.* Ulster, Northern Ireland: Barnardo's

Benson ML and Fox GL (2004) *When Violence Hits Home: How economics and neighborhood play a role.* Washington: National Institute of Justice

Berkowitz SJ and Marans SM (2000) 'The Child Development-Community Policing Program: A partnership to address the impact of violence' *Israel Journal of Psychiatry and Related Sciences* 37 (2) 103-114

Bilby C and Hatcher R (2004) *Early Stages in the Development of the Integrated Domestic Abuse Programme (IDAP): Implementing the Duluth Domestic Violence pathfinder.* (Home Office Online Report 29/04.) London: Home Office. Available online at http://rds.homeoffice.gov.uk/rds/pdfs04/rdsolr2904.pdf

Blodgett C, Behan K, Erp M, Harrington R and Souers K (2008) 'Crisis Intervention for Children and Caregivers Exposed to Intimate Partner Violence' *Best Practice in Mental Health* 4 (1) 74-91

Bogat GA, DeJonghe E, Levendosky AA, Davidson WS and von Eye A (2006) 'Trauma Symptoms among Infants Exposed to Intimate Partner Violence' *Child Abuse and Neglect* 30 (2) 109-125

Booth T and Booth W (1998) 'Think of the Children: Growing up with parents who have learning difficulties' *Journal of Intellectual Disabilities* 2 (3) 138-143

Booth T and Booth W (2002) 'Men in the Lives of Mothers with Intellectual Disabilities' *Journal of Applied Research in Intellectual Disabilities* 15 (3) 187-199

Bowen E, Heron J, Waylen A and Wolke D (2005) 'Domestic Violence Risk During and After Pregnancy: Findings from a British longitudinal study' *BJOG: An International Journal of Obstetrics and Gynaecology* 112 (8) 1083-1089

Boy A and Salihu HM (2004) 'Intimate Partner Violence and Birth Outcomes: A systematic review' *International Journal of Fertility and Women's Medicine* 49 (4) 159-164

Bragg H (2003) *Child Protection in Families Experiencing Domestic Violence.* Washington: Washington Office on Child Abuse and Neglect, Calibre Asssociates

Brandon M, Bailey S, Belderson P, Gardner R, Sidebotham P, Dodsworth J, Warren C and Black J (2009) *Understanding Serious Case Reviews and their Impact: A biennial analysis of serious case reviews 2005-07.* (Research Report No DCSF-RR129.) London: DCSF

Brandon M, Howe A, Dagley V, Salter C and Warren C (2006) 'What Appears to be Helping or Hindering Practitioners in Implementing the Common Assessment Framework and Lead Professional Working?' *Child Abuse Review* 15 (6) 396-413

Brandon M, Thoburn J, Lewis A and Way A (1999) *Safeguarding Children with the Children Act 1989.* London: The Stationery Office

Bream V and Buchanan A (2003) 'Distress among Children whose Separated or Divorced Parents Cannot Agree Arrangements for Them' *British Journal of Social Work* 33 (2) 227-238

Breiding MJ, Black MC and Ryan GW (2008) 'Prevalence and Risk Factors of Intimate Partner Violence in Eighteen US States/Territories, 2005' *American Journal of Public Health* 34 (2) 112-118

Brooks R, Wajsowicz L and Webb E (2002) 'A Comparative Study, Using Focus Groups, of Primary Care Professionals' Attitudes to, and Knowledge of, Domestic Violence and its Impact upon Children' *Archives of Disease in Childhood* 86 (Supplement 1), A53-A54

Brooks R and Webb E (2007) 'Helping Families who are Victims of Domestic Abuse' in Vostanis P (ed), *Mental Health Services and Interventions for Vulnerable Children and Young People.* London: Jessica Kingsley Publishers

Brown A, Cosgrave E, Killackey E, Purcell R, Buckby J and Yung AR (2009) 'The Longitudinal Association of Adolescent Dating Violence with Psychiatric Disorders and Functioning' *Journal of Interpersonal Violence* 24 (12) 1964-1979

Brown T (2006) 'Child Abuse and Domestic Violence in the Context of Parental Separation and Divorce: New models of intervention' in Humphreys C and Stanley N (eds), *Domestic Violence and Child Protection: Directions for good practice.* London: Jessica Kingsley Publishers

Brown T (2010) Personal communication, 27 August 2010

Browne KD and Hamilton CE (1999) 'Police Recognition of the Links between Spouse Abuse and Child Abuse' *Child Maltreatment* 4 (2) 136-147

Brownridge DA (2008) 'Understanding the Elevated Risk of Partner Violence Against Aboriginal Women: A Comparison of two nationally representative surveys of Canada' *Journal of Family Violence* 23 (5) 353-367

Buckley H, Holt S and Whelan S (2006) *Listen to Me! Children's experiences of domestic violence.* Dublin: Children's Research Centre, Trinity College

Buckley H, Holt S and Whelan S (2007) 'Listen to Me! Children's Experiences of Domestic Violence' *Child Abuse Review* 16 (5)

Bullock K, Sarre S, Tarling R and Wilkinson M (2010) *The Delivery of Domestic Abuse Programmes: An implementation study of domestic abuse programmes in probation areas and Her Majesty's Prison Service.* London: Ministry of Justice

Bunston W (2008) 'Baby Lead the Way: Mental health group work for infants, children and mothers affected by family violence' *Journal of Family Studies* 14 (2-3) 334-341

Burman E and Chantler K (2004) 'There's "No Place" Like Home: Emotional geographies of researching "race" and refuge provision in Britain' *Gender, Place and Culture* 11 (3) 375-397

Burman E and Chantler K (2005) 'Domestic Violence and Minoritisation: Legal and policy barriers facing minoritised women leaving violent relationships' *International Journal of Law and Psychiatry* 28 (1) 59-74

Burman E, Smailes SL and Chantler K (2004) '"Culture" as a Barrier to Service Provision and Delivery: Domestic violence services for minoritized women' *Critical Social Policy* 24 (3) 332-357

Burton S, Linda R and Kelly L (1998) *Supporting Women and Challenging Men: Lessons from the Domestic Violence Intervention Project.* Bristol: Policy Press.

Busch R and Robertson N (2000) 'Innovative Approaches to Child Custody and Domestic Violence in New Zealand' *Journal of Aggression, Maltreatment and Trauma* 3 (1) 269-299

Byrne D and Taylor B (2007) 'Children at Risk from Domestic Violence and their Educational Attainment: Perspectives of education welfare officers, social workers and teachers' *Child Care in Practice* 13 (3) 185-201

Calder MC (2009) *Evaluation of Barnardo's Domestic Violence Model in London.* Calder Training and Consultancy. Available online at www.londonscb.gov.uk/files/meetings/dv_seminar/martin_calder_may_13_2009.ppt (Accessed 14 October 2010)

Casanueva C, Martin SL, Runyan DK, Barth R and Bradley RH (2008) 'Quality of Maternal Parenting among Intimate-Partner Violence Victims Involved with the Child Welfare System' *Journal of Family Violence* 23 (6) 413-427

Casey R, Berkman M, Stover CS, Gill K and Durso S (2007) 'Preliminary Results of a Police-Advocate Home-Visit Intervention Project for Victims of Domestic Violence' *Journal of Psychological Trauma* 6 (1) 39-49

Chan YC and Yeung JWK (2009) 'Children Living with Violence within the Family and its Sequel: A meta-analysis from 1995-2006' *Aggression and Violent Behavior* 14 (5) 313-322

Chang JJ, Theodore AD, Martin SL and Runyan DK (2008) 'Psychological Abuse Between Parents: Associations with child maltreatment from a population-based sample' *Child Abuse and Neglect* 32 (8) 819-829

Chantler K, Gangoli G and Hester M (2009) 'Forced Marriage in the UK: Religious, cultural, economic or state violence?' *Critical Social Policy* 29 (4) 587-612

Chemtob CM and Carlson JG (2004) 'Psychological Effects of Domestic Violence on Children and their Mothers' *International Journal of Stress Management* 11 (3) 209-226

Christian CW, Scribano P, Seidl T and Pinto-Martin JA (1997) 'Pediatric Injury Resulting from Family Violence' *Pediatrics* 99 (2) e8

Cleaver H, Nicholson D, Tarr S and Cleaver D (2007) *Child Protection, Domestic Violence and Parental Substance Misuse: Family experiences and effective practice.* London: Jessica Kingsley Publishers

Cleaver H, Unell I and Aldgate J (forthcoming 2011) *The Impact of Parental Mental Illness, Learning Disability, Problem Alcohol and Drug Use and Domestic Violence on Children's Safety and Development.* 2nd edition. London: TSO

Cleaver H and Walker S (2004) 'From Policy to Practice: The implementation of a new framework for social work assessments of children and families' *Child and Family Social Work* 9 (1) 81-90

Cleaver H, Walker S and Meadows P (2004) *Assessing Children's Needs and Circumstances.* London: Jessica Kingsley Publishers

Cleveland HH, Herrera VM and Stuewig J (2003) 'Abusive Males and Abused Females in Adolescent Relationships: Risk factor similarity and dissimilarity and the role of relationship seriousness' *Journal of Family Violence* 18 (6) 325-339

Cohen JA and Mannarino A (2008) 'Trauma-Focused Cognitive Behavioural Therapy for Children and Parents' *Child and Adolescent Mental Health* 13 (4) 158-162

Collin-Vézina D, Hébert M, Manseau H, Blais M and Fernet M (2006) 'Self-Concept and Dating Violence in 220 Adolescent Girls in the Child Protective System' *Child and Youth Care Forum* 35 (4) 319-326

Collishaw S, Pickles, A, Messer J, Rutter M, Shearer C and Maughan B (2007) 'Resilience to Adult Psychopathology Following Childhood Maltreatment: Evidence from a community sample' *Child Abuse and Neglect* 31 (3) 211-230

Coohey C and Frazer C (2006) 'Children and Domestic Violence: A system of safety in clinical practice' *Social Work* 59 (4) 462-473

Cook D, Burton M, Robinsa A and Vallely V (2004) *Evaluation of Specialist Domestic Violence Courts/Fast Track Systems.* London: Crown Prosecution Service, Department for Constitutional Affairs

Corso PS and Fertig AR (2010) 'The Economic Impact of Child Maltreatment in the United States: Are the estimates credible?' *Child Abuse and Neglect* 34 (5) 296-304

Cox CE, Kotch JB and Everson MD (2003) 'A Longitudinal Study of Modifying Influences in the Relationship Between Domestic Violence and Child Maltreatment' *Journal of Family Violence* 18 (1) 5-17

Craig G and Stanley N (2006) 'Young People's Use of Sexual Health Services in Rural Areas' *Children and Society* 20 (3) 171-182

Cross TP, Finkelhor D and Ormrod R (2005) 'Police Involvement in Child Protective Services Investigations: Literature review and secondary data analysis' *Child Maltreatment* 10 (3) 224-244

Cummings EM, El-Sheikh M, Kouros CD and Buckhalt JA (2009) 'Children and Violence: The role of children's regulation in the marital aggression–child adjustment link' *Clinical Child and Family Psychology Review* 12 (1) 3-15

Cunningham A and Baker L (2004) *What About Me! Seeking to understand a child's view of violence in the family.* London, Ontario: Centre for Children and Families in the Justice System

Cunningham A and Baker L (2009) 'Inter-Parental Violence: The pre-schooler's perspective and the educator's role' *Early Childhood Education Journal* 37 (3) 199-207

Damant D, Lapierre S, Lebosse C, Thibault S, Lessard G, Hamelin-Brabant L, Lavergne C and Fortin A (2010) 'Women's Abuse of their Children in the Context of Domestic Violence: Reflection from women's accounts' *Child and Family Social Work* 15 (1) 12-21

Daniel B and Wassell S (2002) *Adolescence: Assessing and promoting resilience in vulnerable children 3.* London: Jessica Kingsley Publishers

D'Cruz H (2002) 'Constructing the Identities of "Responsible Mothers, Invisible Men" in Child Protection Practice' *Sociological Research Online* 7 (1)

DCSF News (2009) 'New Guidance Issued as Reports of Forced Marriage Increase', 2nd July, available online at www.dcsf.gov.uk/pns/DisplayPN.cgi%3Fpn_id%3D2009_0123 (Accessed 10 September 2010)

Debbonaire T (2007) *An Evaluation of the Sutton Stronger Families Group Programme for Children Exposed to Domestic Violence. Executive summary of the findings.* (Unpublished report.) London: London Borough of Sutton

Debbonaire T (2010) *Respect Briefing Paper: Evidence of effects of domestic violence perpetrator programmes on women's safety.* London: Respect. Available online at www.respect.uk.net/data/files/resources/respect_briefing_paper_on_the_evidence_of_effects_of_perpetrator_programmes_on_women_revised_18th_march_10.pdf (Accessed 21 August 2010)

Debbonaire T and Westminster Domestic Violence Forum (2002) *Domestic Violence Prevention Pack for Schools.* London: WDVF

DeGue S and DiLillo D (2009) 'Is Animal Cruelty a "Red Flag" for Family Violence?: Investigating co-occurring violence toward children, partners, and pets' *Journal of Interpersonal Violence* 24 (6) 1036-1056

Department for Children Schools and Families and Department of Health (2010) *Keeping Children and Young People in Mind: The government's full response to the Independent Review of CAMHS.* Nottingham: DCSF

Department of Health (2005) *Responding to Domestic Abuse: A handbook for health professionals.* London: Department of Health

Devaney J (2008) 'Chronic Child Abuse and Domestic Violence: Children and families with long-term and complex needs' *Child and Family Social Work* 13 (4) 443-453

Devaney J and Spratt T (2009) 'Child Abuse as a Complex and Wicked Problem: Reflecting on policy developments in the United Kingdom in working with children and families with multiple problems' *Children and Youth Services Review* 31 (6) 635-641

Dobash RP, Dobash RE, Cavanagh K and Lewis R (1999) 'A Research Evaluation of British Programmes for Violent Men' *Journal of Social Policy* 28 (2) 205-233

Donovan C, Griffiths S, Groves N, Johnson H and Douglass J (2010) *Evaluation of Early Intervention Models for Change in Domestic Violence: Northern Rock Foundation Domestic Abuse Intervention Project, 2004–2009.* Newcastle upon Tyne: Northern Rock Foundation

Donovan C and Hester M (2010) '"I Hate the Word 'Victim'": An exploration of recognition of domestic violence in same-sex relationships' *Social Policy and Society* 9 (2) 279-289

Donovan RJ and Vlais R (2005) *VicHealth Review of Communication Components of Social Marketing/Public Education Campaigns Focusing on Violence Against Women.* Melbourne: Victorian Health Promotion Foundation

Dorkenoo E, Morison L and Macfarlane A (2007) *A Statistical Study to Estimate the Prevalence of Female Genital Mutilation in England and Wales: Summary report.* London: Foundation for Women's Health, Research and Development (FORWARD)

Downs WR and Miller BA (2002) 'Treating Dual Problems of Partner Violence and Substance Abuse' in Wekerle C and Wall A (eds), *The Violence and Addiction Equation: Theoretical and clinical issues in substance abuse and relationship violence.* Hove: Brunner-Routledge

Dubowitz H, Black MM, Kerr MA, Morrel TM, Hussey JM, Everson MD and Starr Jr RH (2001) 'Type and Timing of Mothers' Victimization: Effects on Mothers and Children' *Pediatrics* 107 (4) 728-735

Eaves (2009) *Soujourner Service Information,* available online at www.eaves4women. co.uk/Documents/Press%20releases/SoujournerServiceInformation.pdf (Accessed 22 July 2010)

Eckenrode J, Ganzel B, Henderson CR Jr, Smith E, Olds DL, Powers J, Cole R, Kitzman H and Sidora K (2000) 'Preventing Child Abuse and Neglect with a Program of Nurse Home Visitation: The limiting effects of domestic violence' *Journal of the American Medical Association* 284 (11) 1385-1391

Edleson JL (1998) 'Responsible Mothers and Invisible Men: Child protection in the case of adult domestic violence' *Journal of Interpersonal Violence* 13 (2) 294-298

Edleson JL (1999a) 'Children's Witnessing of Adult Domestic Violence' *Journal of Interpersonal Violence* 14 (8) 839-870

Edleson JL (1999b) 'The Overlap between Child Maltreatment and Woman Battering' *Violence Against Women* 5 (2) 134-154

Edleson JL (2004) 'Should Childhood Exposure to Adult Domestic Violence be Defined as Child Maltreatment under the Law?' in Jaffe PG, Baker LL and Cunningham AJ (eds), *Protecting Children from Domestic Violence: Strategies for community intervention.* New York: Guilford Press

Edleson JL and Malik NM (2008) 'Collaborating for Family Safety' *Journal of Interpersonal Violence* 23 (7) 871-875

Edleson JL, Mbilinyi LF, Beeman SK and Hagemeister AK (2003) 'How Children Are Involved in Adult Domestic Violence: Results from a four-city telephone survey' *Journal of Interpersonal Violence* 18 (1) 18-32

Eley S (2005) 'Changing Practices: The specialised domestic violence court process' *Howard Journal of Criminal Justice* 44 (2) 113-124

Ellis J (2004) *Preventing Violence Against Women and Girls. A study of educational programmes for children and young people.* London: WOMANKIND Worldwide

Ellis J (2008) 'Primary Prevention of Domestic Abuse through Education' in Humphreys C, Houghton C and Ellis J (eds), *Literature Review: Better Outcomes for Children and Young People Experiencing Domestic Abuse – Directions for good practice.* Edinburgh: Scottish Executive

English DJ, Edleson JL and Herrick ME (2005) 'Domestic Violence in One State's Child Protective Caseload: A study of differential case dispositions and outcomes' *Children and Youth Services Review* 27 (11) 1183-1201

English DJ, Marshall DB and Stewart AJ (2003) 'Effects of Family Violence on Child Behavior and Health During Early Childhood' *Journal of Family Violence* 18 (1) 43-57

English DJ, Wingard T, Marshall D, Orme M and Orme A (2000) 'Alternative Responses to Child Protective Services: Emerging issues and concerns' *Child Abuse and Neglect* 24 (3) 375-388

Eriksson M (2009) 'Girls and Boys as Victims: Social workers' approaches to children exposed to violence' *Child Abuse Review* 18 (6) 428-445

Ernst AA, Weiss SJ, Enright-Smith S and Hansen P (2008) 'Positive Outcomes from an Immediate and Ongoing Intervention for Child Witnesses of Intimate Partner Violence' *The American Journal of Emergency Medicine* 26 (4)

Evans SE, Davies C and DeLillo D (2008) 'Exposure to Domestic Violence: A meta-analysis of child and adolescent outcomes' *Aggression and Violent Behavior* 13 (2) 131-140

Faller KC (2003) 'Research and Practice in Child Interviewing: Implications for children exposed to domestic violence' *Journal of Interpersonal Violence* 18 (4) 377-389

Farmer E (2006) 'Using Research to Develop Practice in Child Protection and Child Care' in Humphreys C and Stanley N (eds), *Domestic Violence and Child Protection: Directions for good practice*. London: Jessica Kingsley Publishers

Farmer E and Owen M (1995) *Child Protection Practice: Private risks and public remedies*. London: The Stationery Office

Featherstone B (2009) *Contemporary Fathering: Theory, policy and practice*. Bristol: Policy Press

Featherstone B and Peckover S (2007) 'Letting Them Get Away With It: Fathers, domestic violence and child welfare' *Critical Social Policy* 27 (2) 181-202

Fieggen AG, Wiemann M, Brown C, van As AB, Swingler GH and Peter JC (2004) 'Inhuman Shields – Children caught in the crossfire of domestic violence' *South African Medical Journal* 94 (4) 293-296

Field CA and Caetano R (2004) 'Ethnic Difference in Intimate Partner Violence in the US General Population: The role of alcohol use and socioeconomic status' *Trauma, Violence and Abuse* 5 (4) 303-317

Findlater JE and Kelly S (1999) 'Child Protection Services and Domestic Violence' *The Future of Children* 9 (3) 84-95

Finkelhor D, Ormrod R, Turner H (2007a) 'Poly-victimization: A neglected component in child victimization trauma' *Child Abuse and Neglect* 31 (1) 7-26

Finkelhor D, Ormrod R, Turner H (2007b) 'Revictimization Patterns in a National Longitudinal Sample of Children and Youth' *Child Abuse and Neglect* 31 (5) 479-502

Finkelhor D, Ormrod RK and Turner HA (2009a) 'Lifetime Assessment of Poly-victimization in a National Sample of Children and Youth' *Child Abuse and Neglect* 33 (7) 403-411

Finkelhor D, Ormrod RK, Turner HA and Hamby SL (2005) 'Measuring Poly-victimization using the JVQ' *Child Abuse and Neglect* 29 (11) 1297-1312

Finkelhor D, Turner H, Ormrod R and Hamby S (2009b) 'Violence, Abuse, and Crime Exposure in a National Sample of Children and Youth' *Pediatrics* 124 (5) 1411-1423

Finney A (2004) *Alcohol and Intimate Partner Violence: Key findings from the research*. London: Home Office

Fisher H (forthcoming 2011) 'The Overall Impact' in Radford L, Corral S, Bradley C, Fisher H, Bassett C and Howat N, with Collishaw S, *The Maltreatment and Victimisation of Children in the UK: NSPCC report on a national survey of young peoples', young adults' and caregivers' experiences*. London: NSPCC

Foreign and Commonwealth Office, Scottish Executive and Home Office (2006) *Forced Marriage: A wrong not a right*. London: Community Liaison Unit, Foreign and Commonwealth Office

Forrester D and Harwin J (2008) 'Parental Substance Misuse and Child Welfare: Outcomes for children two years after referral' *British Journal of Social Work* 38 (8) 1518-1535

Foshee VA, Bauman KE, Arriaga XB, Helms RW, Koch GG and Linder GF (1998) 'An Evaluation of Safe Dates, an Adolescent Dating Violence Prevention Program' *American Journal of Public Health* 88 (1) 45-50

Foshee VA, Bauman KE, Ennett ST, Linder F, Benefield T and Suchindran C (2004) 'Assessing the Long-term Effects of the Safe Dates Program and a Booster in Preventing and Reducing Adolescent Dating Violence Victimization and Perpetration' *American Journal of Public Health* 94 (4) 619-624

Foshee VA, Bauman KE, Greene WF, Koch GG, Linder GF and MacDougall JE (2000) 'The Safe Dates Program: 1-year follow-up results' *American Journal of Public Health* 90 (10) 1619-1622

Foshee VA, Linder GF, Bauman KE, Langwick SA, Arriaga XB, Heath JL, McMahon PM and Bangdiwala S (1996) 'The Safe Dates Project: Theoretical basis, evaluation design, and selected baseline findings' *American Journal of Preventative Medicine* 12 (2) 39-47

Fowler DN and Chanmugam A (2007) 'A Critical Review of Quantitative Analyses of Children Exposed to Domestic Violence: Lessons for practice and research' *Brief Treatment and Crisis Intervention* 7 (4) 322-344

Fox GL and Benson ML (2004) 'Violent Men, Bad Dads? Fathering profiles of men involved in intimate partner violence' in Day RD and Lamb ME (eds), *Conceptualizing and Measuring Father Involvement.* Mahwah, NJ: Lawrence Erlbaum

Galvani S (2004) 'Responsible Disinhibition: Alcohol, men and violence to women' *Addiction Research and Theory* 12 (4) 357-371

Galvani S (2006) 'Safety First? The impact of domestic abuse on women's treatment experience' *Journal of Substance Abuse* 11 (6) 395-407

Gangoli G, McCarry M and Razak A (2009) 'Child Marriage or Forced Marriage? South Asian communities in North East England' *Children and Society* 23 (6) 418-429

Gerwitz AH and Edleson JL (2007) 'Young Children's Exposure to Intimate Partner Violence: Towards a developmental risk and resilience framework for research and intervention' *Journal of Family Violence* 22 (3) 151-163

Ghate D and Hazel N (2002) *Parenting in Poor Environments: Stress, support and coping.* London: Jessica Kingsley Publishers

Gilchrist E, Johnson RT, Weston S, Beech A and Kebbell M (2003) *Domestic Violence Offenders: Characteristics and offending related needs.* Findings 217. London: Home Office

Gill AK and Mitra-Kahn T (2010) '"Moving towards a Multiculturalism without Culture": Constructing a victim-friendly human rights approach to forced marriage in the UK' in Thiara RK and Gill AK (eds), *Violence Against Women in South Asian Communities: Issues for policy and practice.* London: Jessica Kingsley Publishers

Goddard C and Bedi G (2010) 'Intimate Partner Violence and Child Abuse: A child-centred perspective' *Child Abuse Review* 19 (1) 5-20

Gondolf EW (2000) '30-month Follow-up of Court-referred Batterers in Four Cities' *International Journal of Offender Therapy and Comparative Criminology* 44 (1) 41-61

Gondolf EW (2002) *Batterer Intervention Systems: Issues, outcomes, and recommendations.* Thousand Oaks, CA: Sage Publications

Gondolf EW (2004) 'Evaluating Batterer Counseling Programs: A difficult task showing some effects and implications' *Aggression and Violent Behavior* 9 (6) 605-631

Gorin S (2004) *Understanding What Children Say: Children's experiences of domestic violence, parental substance misuse and parental health problems.* London: National Children's Bureau and NSPCC

Graham-Bermann SA (1996) 'Family Worries: Assessment of interpersonal anxiety in children from violent and nonviolent families' *Journal of Clinical Child Psychology* 25 (3) 280-287

Graham-Bermann SA, Gruber G, Howell KH and Girz L (2009) 'Factors Discriminating among Profiles of Resilience and Psychopathology in Children Exposed to Intimate Partner Violence (IPV)' *Child Abuse and Neglect* 33 (9) 648-660

Graham-Bermann SA and Levendosky AA (1998) 'Traumatic Stress Symptoms in Children of Battered Women' *Journal of Interpersonal Violence* 13 (1) 111-129

Graham-Bermann SA, Lynch SA, Banyard V, DeVoe ER and Halabu H (2007) 'Community-based Intervention for Children Exposed to Intimate Partner Violence: An efficacy trial' *Journal of Consulting and Clincial Psychology* 75 (2) 199-209

Graham-Bermann SA and Seng J (2005) 'Violence Exposure and Traumatic Stress Symptoms as Additional Predictors of Health Problems in High-risk Children' *The Journal of Pediatrics* 146 (3) 349-354

Gray B (2003) 'Social Exclusion, Poverty, Health and Social Care in Tower Hamlets: The perspectives of families on the impact of the Family Support Service' *British Journal of Social Work* 33 (3) 361-380

Gregory A, Ramsay J, Agnew-Davies R, Baird K, Devine A, Dunne D, Eldridge S, Howell A, Johnson M, Rutterford C, Sharp D and Feder G (2010) 'Primary care Identification and Referral to Improve Safety of women experiencing domestic violence (IRIS): Protocol for a pragmatic cluster randomised controlled trial' *BMC Public Health* 10:54

Grych JH, Jouriles EN, Swank PR, McDonald R and Norwood WD (2000) 'Patterns of Adjustment among Children of Battered Women' *Journal of Consulting and Clinical Psychology* 68 (1) 84-94

Guille L (2004) 'Men who Batter and their Children: An integrated review' *Aggression and Violent Behavior* 9 (2) 129-163

Guru S (2006) 'Working with Asian Perpetrators of Domestic Violence – The British experience' *Practice* 18 (3) 153-166

Gutierres SE and Van Puymbroeck C (2006) 'Childhood and Adult Violence in the Lives of Women who Misuse Substances' *Aggression and Violent Behavior* 11 (5) 497-513

Hague G, Kelly L, Malos E and Mullender A, with Debbonaire T (1996) *Children, Domestic Violence and Refuges: A study of needs and responses.* Bristol: Women's Aid Federation of England

Hague G and Malos E (1998) 'Inter-agency Approaches to Domestic Violence and the Role of Social Services' *British Journal of Social Work* 28 (3) 369-386

Hague G, Thiara R, Magowan P and Mullender A (2008) *Making the Links: Disabled women and domestic violence.* London: Women's Aid

Hampshire Constabulary (2007) *North and East OCU Analyst Report.* (Unpublished report.) Winchester: Hampshire Constabulary

Harne L (2004) 'Childcare, Violence and Fathering – Are violent fathers who look after their children likely to be less abusive?' in Klein R and Wallner B (eds), *Gender, Conflict and Violence.* Vienna: Studien-Verlag

Harrison C (2006) 'Dammed If You Do and Dammed If You Don't? The contradictions between private and public law' in Humphreys C and Stanley N (eds), *Domestic Violence and Child Protection: Directions for good practice.* London: Jessica Kingsley Publishers

Hartley CC (2004) 'Severe Domestic Violence and Child Maltreatment: Considering child physical abuse, neglect, and failure to protect' *Child and Youth Services Review* 26 (4) 373-392

Harvey A, Garcia-Moreno C and Butchart A (2007) *Primary Prevention of Intimate-partner Violence and Sexual Violence: Background paper for WHO expert meeting May 2–3.* Geneva: World Health Organisation

Hegar R and Greif G (1991) 'Parental Kidnapping across International Borders' *International Social Work* 34 (4) 353-363

Hendry EB (1998) 'Children and Domestic Violence: A training imperative' *Child Abuse Review* 7 (2) 129-134

Herrenkohl T, Sousa C, Tajima E, Herrenkohl R and Moylan C (2008) 'Intersection of Child Abuse and Children's Exposure to Domestic Violence' *Trauma, Violence, and Abuse* 9 (2) 84-99

Hester M (2004) 'Future Trends and Developments – Violence against women in Europe and East Asia' *Violence Against Women* 10 (12) 1431-1448

Hester M (2005) 'Tackling Men's Violence in Families: Lessons for England' in Eriksson M, Hester M, Keskinen S and Pringle K (eds), *Tackling Men's Violence in Families: Nordic issues and dilemmas.* Bristol: Policy Press

Hester M (2006) 'Asking about Domestic Violence: Implications for practice' in Humphreys C and Stanley N (eds), *Domestic Violence and Child Protection: Directions for good practice.* London: Jessica Kingsley Publishers

Hester M (2009) *Who Does What to Whom? Gender and domestic violence perpetrators.* Bristol: University of Bristol, in association with the Northern Rock Foundation

Hester M, Pearce J and Westmarland N (2008) *Early Evaluation of the Integrated Domestic Violence Court, Croydon.* (Ministry of Justice Research Series 18/08.) London: Ministry of Justice

Hester M and Pearson C (1998) *From Periphery to Centre – Domestic violence in work with abused children.* Bristol: Policy Press

Hester M, Pearson C, Harwin N and Abrahams H (2007) *Making an Impact: Children and domestic violence, a reader. 2nd edition.* London: Jessica Kingsley Publishers

Hester M and Radford L (1996) *Domestic Violence and Child Contact Arrangements in England and Denmark.* Bristol: Policy Press

Hester M and Westmarland N (2005) *Tackling Domestic Violence: Effective interventions and approaches.* (Home Office Research Study 290.) London: Home Office Research, Development and Statistics Directorate

Hester M, Westmarland N, Gangoli G, Wilkinson M, O'Kelly C, Kent A and Diamond A (2006) *Domestic Violence Perpetrators: Identifying needs to inform early intervention.* Bristol: University of Bristol

HM Government (2010) *The Right to Choose: Multi-Agency Statutory Guidance for Dealing with Forced Marriage.* 2nd edition. London: Forced Marriage Unit HM Government

HMICA (HM Inspectorate of Court Administration) (2005) *Domestic Violence, Safety and Family Proceedings.* Bristol: HMICA

Hocking J (2007) 'Safety in Numbers' *Community Care* 1 February

Holden GW (2003) 'Children Exposed to Domestic Violence and Child Abuse: Terminology and taxonomy' *Clinical Child and Family Psychology Review* 6 (3) 151-160

Holden GW, Stein JD, Richie KL, Harris SD and Jouriles EN (1998) 'Parenting Behaviour and Beliefs of Battered Women' in Holden GW, Geffner R and Jouriles EN (eds), *Children Exposed to Marital Violence: Theory, research, and applied issues.* Washington, DC: American Psychological Association

Holt S (2003) 'Child Protection Work and Men's Abuse of Women: An Irish study' *Child and Family Social Work* 8 (1) 53-65

Holt S, Buckley H and Whelan S (2008) 'The Impact of Exposure to Domestic Violence on Children and Young People: A review of the literature' *Child Abuse and Neglect* 32 (8) 797-810

Howard LM, Trevillion K, Khalifeh H, Woodall A, Agnew-Davies R and Feder G (2009) 'Domestic Violence and Severe Psychiatric Disorders: Prevalence and interventions' *Psychological Medicine* 40 (6) 881-893

Howarth E, Stimpson L, Barran D and Robinson A (2009) *Safety in Numbers: A multi-site evaluation of Independent Domestic Violence Advisor Services.* London: The Henry Smith Charity

Howells NL and Rosenbaum A (2008) 'Examination of Sex Differences and Type of Violence Exposure in a Mediation Model of Family Violence' *Journal of Emotional Abuse* 8 (1-2) 123-138

Hoyle C (2008) 'Will She Be Safe? A critical analysis of risk assessment in domestic violence cases' *Children and Youth Services Review* 30 (3) 323-337

Hulbert SN (2008) 'Children Exposed to Violence in the Child Protection System: Practice-based assessment of the system process can lead to practical strategies for improvement' *Journal of Emotional Abuse* 8 (1-2) 217-234

Humphreys C (1999) Avoidance and Confrontation: Social work practice in relation to domestic violence and child abuse' *Child and Family Social Work* 4 (1) 77-87

Humphreys C (2007) 'Domestic Violence and Child Protection: Exploring the role of perpetrator risk assessments' *Child and Family Social Work* 12 (4) 360-369

Humphreys C (2008) 'Problems in the system of mandatory reporting of children living with domestic violence' *Journal of Family Studies* 14 (2) 228-239

Humphreys C, Houghton C and Ellis J (eds) (2008) *Literature Review: Better Outcomes for Children and Young People Experiencing Domestic Abuse – Directions for good practice.* Edinburgh: Scottish Executive

Humphreys C, Lowe P and Williams S (2009) 'Sleep Disruption and Domestic Violence: Exploring the interconnections between mothers and children' *Child and Family Social Work* 14 (1) 6-14

Humphreys C and Mullender A (2000) *Children and Domestic Violence: A research overview of the impact on children*. Dartington: research in practice

Humphreys C, Mullender A, Lowe P, Hague G, Abrahams H and Hester M (2001) 'Domestic Violence and Child Abuse: Developing sensitive policies and guidance' *Child Abuse Review* 10 (3) 183-197

Humphreys C, Regan L, River D and Thiara R (2005) 'Domestic Violence and Substance Use: Tackling complexity' *British Journal of Social Work* 35 (8) 1303-1320

Humphreys C and Thiara R (2003) 'Domestic Violence and Mental Health: "I call it symptoms of abuse"' *British Journal of Social Work* 33 (2) 209-26

Humphreys C, Thiara R, Mullender A and Skamballis A (2006a) '"Talking to My Mum": Developing communication between mothers and children in the aftermath of domestic violence' *Journal of Social Work* 6 (1) 53-63

Humphreys C, Thiara R, Skamballis A and Mullender A (2006b) *Talking About Domestic Abuse: A photo activity workbook to develop communication between mothers and young people*. London: Jessica Kingsley Publishers

Humphreys C, Thiara R, Skamballis A and Mullender A (2006c) *Talking to My Mum: A picture workbook for workers, mothers and children affected by domestic abuse*. London: Jessica Kingsley Publishers

Huth-Bocks A, Schettini A and Shebroe V (2001) 'Group Play Therapy for Preschoolers Exposed to Domestic Violence' *Journal of Child and Adolescent Group Therapy* 11 (1) 19-34

Israel E and Stover C (2009) 'Intimate Partner Violence: The role of the relationship between perpetrators and children who witness violence' *Journal of Interpersonal Violence* 24 (10) 1755-1764

Izzidien S (2008) *'I Can't Tell People what is Happening at Home.' Domestic abuse within South Asian communities: the specific needs of women, children and young people*. London: NSPCC. Available online at www.nspcc.org.uk/Inform/research/ Findings/ICantTell_wda57838.html (Accessed 15 July 2010)

Jack G (2004) 'Child Protection at the Community Level' *Child Abuse Review* 13 (6) 368-383

Jaffe PG and Juodis M (2006) 'Children as Victims and Witnesses of Domestic Homicide: Lessons learned from domestic violence death review committees' *Juvenile and Family Court Journal* 57 (3) 13–28

Jaffe PG, Lemon NKD and Poisson SE (2003) *Child Custody and Domestic Violence: A call for safety and accountability*. Thousand Oaks, CA: Sage

Jaffe PG, Suderman M, Reitzel and Killip SM (1992) 'An Evaluation of a Secondary School Primary Prevention Program on Violence in Intimate Relationships' *Violence and Victims* 7 (2) 129-146

Jaffee SR, Caspi A, Moffitt TE, Polo-Tomás M and Taylor A (2007) 'Individual, Family, and Neighborhood Factors Distinguish Resilient from Non-resilient Maltreated Children: A cumulative stressors model' *Child Abuse and Neglect* 31 (3) 231-53

Jasinski JL (2004) 'Pregnancy and Domestic Violence: A review of the literature' *Trauma, Violence, and Abuse* 5 (1) 47-64

Johnson M (2010) '"Herding Cats": The experiences of domestic violence advocates engaging with primary care providers' *Safe: The Domestic Abuse Quarterly* 32 (Winter) 14-17

Johnson SP and Sullivan CM (2008) 'How Child Protection Workers Support or Further Victimize Battered Mothers' *Affilia* 23 (3) 242-257

Johnston JR (2006) 'A Child-Centered Approach to High-Conflict and Domestic-Violence Families: Differential assessment and interventions' *Journal of Family Studies* 12 (1) 15-35

Johnston JR, Sagatun-Edwards I, Blomquist ME and Girdner LK (2000) *Prevention of Family Abduction through Early Identification of Risk Factors.* Washington, DC: Office of Juvenile Justice and Deliquency Prevention, US Department of Justice

Jones LP, Gross E and Becker I (2002) 'The Characteristics of Domestic Violence Victims in a Child Protective Service Caseload' *Families in Society* 83 (4) 405-415

Kaslow NJ and Thompson MP (2008) 'Associations of Child Maltreatment and Intimate Partner Violence with Psychological Adjustment among Low SES, African American Children' *Child Abuse and Neglect* 32 (9) 888-896

Kazimirski A, Keogh P, Kumari V, Smith R, Gowland S and Purdon S, with Khanum N (National Centre for Social Research) (2009) *Forced Marriage: Prevalence and service response.* (Research Report No DCSF-RR128.) London: Department for Children, Schools and Families

Kelleher I, Harley M, Lynch F, Arseneault L, Fitzpatrick C and Cannon M (2008a) 'Associations between Childhood Trauma, Bullying and Psychotic Symptoms among a School-based Adolescent Sample' *The British Journal of Psychiatry* 193 (5) 378-382

Kelleher KJ, Hazen AL, Coben JH, Wang Y, McGeehan J, Kohl PL and Gardner WP (2008b) 'Self-reported Disciplinary Practices among Women in the Child Welfare System: Association with domestic violence victimization' *Child Abuse and Neglect* 32 (8) 811-818

Kellog ND and Menard SW (2003) 'Violence among Family Members of Children and Adolescents Evaluated for Sexual Abuse' *Child Abuse and Neglect* 27 (12) 1367 - 1376

Khanum N (2008) *Forced Marriage, Family Cohesion and Community Engagement: National learning through a case study of Luton.* Luton: Equality in Diversity

Kitzmann KM, Gaylord NK, Holt AR and Kenny ED (2003) 'Child Witnesses to Domestic Violence: A meta-analytic review' *Journal of Consulting and Clinical Psychology* 71 (2) 339–52

Laming H (2009) *The Protection of Children in England: A progress report.* London: The Stationery Office

Lapierre S (2010) 'Striving to be "Good" Mothers: Abused women's experiences of mothering' *Child Abuse Review* 19 (5) 342-357

Lazenbatt A and Greer J (2009) 'Safeguarding and Protecting Children in Maternity Services: Implications for practice' *Child Care in Practice* 15 (4) 313-326

Lee HY, Lightfoot E and Edleson JL (2008) 'Differences among Battered Mothers in their Involvement with Child Protection Services: Could the perpetrator's biological relationship to the child have an impact?' *Children and Youth Services Review* 30 (10) 1189-1197

Leonard K (2001) 'Domestic Violence and Alcohol: What is known and what do we need to know to encourage environmental interventions?' *Journal of Substance Misuse* 6 (4) 235-247

Letourneau NL, Fedick CB and Willms JD (2007) 'Mothering and Domestic Violence: A longitudinal analysis' *Journal of Family Violence* 22 (8) 649-659

Levendosky A and Graham-Bermann S (2000) 'Behavioral Observations of Parenting in Battered Women' *Journal of Family Psychology* 14 (1) 80-94

Levendosky A and Graham-Bermann S (2001) 'Parenting in Battered Women: The effects of domestic violence on women and their children' *Journal of Family Violence* 16 (2) 171-192

Levendosky A, Huth-Bocks AC, Shapiro DL and Semel M (2003) 'The Impact of Domestic Abuse on the Maternal-Child Relationship and Pre-school Age Children's Functioning' *Journal of Family Psychology* 17 (3) 275-287

Lewis G (2005) 'Coincidental Deaths and Domestic Violence' in Lewis G and Driffe J (eds), *Why Mothers Die 2000–2002: The sixth report of the Confidential Enquiries into Maternal Deaths in the United Kingdom.* London: Royal College of Obstetricians and Gynaecologists

Lewis G and Driffe J (2001) *Why Mothers Die 1997-1999: The fifth report of the Confidential Enquiries into Maternal Deaths in the United Kingdom.* London: Royal College of Obstetricians and Gynaecologists

Lieberman AF, Van Horn P and Ippen CG (2005) 'Towards Evidence-based Treatment: Child-parent psychotherapy with pre-schoolers exposed to marital violence' *Journal of the American Academy of Child and Adolescent Psychiatry* 44 (12) 1241-8

Lipsky S, Holt VL, Easterling TR and Critchlow CW (2003) 'Impact of Police-reported Intimate Partner Violence During Pregnancy on Birth Outcomes' *Obstetrics and Gynecology* 102 (3) 557-564

Littlechild B and Bourke C (2006) 'Men's Use of Violence and Intimidation Against Family Members and Child Protection Workers' in Humphreys C and Stanley N (eds), *Domestic Violence and Child Protection.* London: Jessica Kingsley Publishers

London Borough of Islington (1994) STOP: *Striving to Prevent Domestic Violence – Resource for working with children and young people.* London: LBI, Women's Equality Unit

London Safeguarding Children Board (2008) *Safeguarding Children Abused Through Domestic Violence.* London: LSCB. Available online at www.londonscb.gov.uk/files/procedures/dv/dv_risk_assessment_matrix__final.pdf (Accessed 21 August 2010)

Lundy M and Grossman SF (2005) 'The Mental Health and Service Needs of Young Children Exposed to Domestic Violence: Supportive data' *Families in Society* 86 (1) 17-29

Lupton C and Nixon P (1999) Empowering Practice? *A critical appraisal of the Family Group Conference approach.* Bristol: The Policy Press

Luthra R, Abramovitz R, Greenberg R, Schoor A, Newcorn J, Schmeidler J, Levine P, Nomura Y and Chemtob CM (2009) 'Relationship Between Type of Trauma Exposure and Posttraumatic Stress Disorder among Urban Children and Adolescents' *Journal of Interpersonal Violence* 24 (11) 1919-1927

Macdonald G (2010) 'Domestic Violence, Children's Voices and Child Contact: Exploring Cafcass Section 7 welfare reports (England).' (Presentation at the annual conference of the Socio-Legal Studies Association, University of the West of England, Bristol.)

MacLeod P, Kinver A, Page L, Iliasov A and Williams R (2009) *2008-09 Scottish Crime and Justice Survey – Partner abuse.* Edinburgh: The Scottish Government

MacMillan HL, Wathen N, Barlow J, Fergusson DM, Leventhal JM and Taussig HN (2009) 'Interventions to Prevent Child Maltreatment and Associated Impairment' *The Lancet* 373 (9659) 250-66

Magen RH (1999) 'In the Best Interests of Battered Women: Reconceptualizing allegations of failure to protect' *Child Maltreatment* 4 (2) 127-135

Magen RH, Conroy K and Del Tufo A (2000) 'Domestic Violence in Child Welfare Preventative Services: Results from an intake screening questionnaire' *Children and Youth Services Review* 22 (3-4) 174–251

Mama A (2001) 'Violence Against Black Women in the Home' in Hanmer J and Itzin C (eds), *Home Truths about Domestic Violence: Feminist influences on policy and practice – A reader.* London: Routledge

Margolin G (2005) 'Children's Exposure to Violence: Exploring developmental pathways to diverse outcomes' *Journal of Interpersonal Violence* 20 (1) 72-81

Margolin G and Gordis EB (2000) 'The Effects of Family and Community Violence on Children' *Annual Review of Psychology* Vol. 51: 445-479

Marie D, Fergusson DM and Boden JM (2008) 'Ethnic Identity and Intimate Partner Violence in a New Zealand Birth Cohort' *Social Policy Journal of New Zealand* 33 (March) 126-145

Martin SG (2002) 'Children Exposed to Domestic Violence: Psychological considerations for health care practitioners' *Holistic Nursing Practice* 16 (3) 7-15

Maynard M (1985) 'The Response of Social Workers to Domestic Violence' in Pahl J (ed), *Private Violence and Public Policy.* London: Routledge and Kegan Paul

McCarry M (2009) 'Justifications and Contradictions: Understanding young people's views of domestic abuse' *Men and Masculinities* 11 (3) 325-345

McCloskey LA and Bailey JA (2000) 'The Intergenerational Transmission of Risk for Child Sexual Abuse' *Journal of Interpersonal Violence* 15 (10) 1019-1035

McCloskey LA and Lichter EL (2003) 'The Contribution of Marital Violence to Adolescent Aggression Across Different Relationships' *Journal of Interpersonal Violence* 18 (4) 390-412

McDonald R, Jouriles EN and Skopp NA (2006) 'Reducing Conduct Problems among Children brought to Women's Shelters: Intervention effects 24 months following termination of services' *Journal of Family Psychology* 20 (1) 127-136

McFarlane JM, Groff JY, O'Brien JA and Watson K (2005) 'Behaviors of Children Following a Randomized Controlled Treatment Program for their Abused Mothers' *Issues in Comprehensive Pediatric Nursing* 28 (4) 195-211

McFarlane JM, Parker B, Soeken K, Silva C and Reel S (1998) 'Safety Behaviors of Abused Women After an Intervention During Pregnancy' *Journal of Obstetric, Gynecologic, and Neonatal Nursing* 27 (1) 64-69

McGee C (1997) 'Children's Experiences of Domestic Violence' *Child and Family Social Work* 2 (1) 13-23

McGee C (2000) *Childhood Experiences of Domestic Violence.* London: Jessica Kingsley Publishers

Meetoo V and Mirza HS (2007) '"There is Nothing 'Honourable' about Honour Killings": Gender, violence and the limits of multiculturalism' *Women's Studies International Forum* 30 (3) 187-200

Meltzer H, Doos L, Vostanis P, Ford T and Goodman R (2009) 'The Mental Health of Children Who Witness Domestic Violence' *Child and Family Social Work* 14 (4) 491-501

Mertin P and Mohr PB (2002) 'Incidence and Correlates of Postrauma Symptoms in Children from Backgrounds of Domestic Violence' *Violence and Victims* 17 (5) 555-567

Miller BA, Downs WR and Gondoli DM (1989) 'Spousal Violence among Alcoholic Women as Compared to a Random Household Sample of Women' *Journal of Studies on Alcohol* 50 (6) 533-540

Mitchell KJ and Finkelhor D (2001) 'Risk of Crime Victimization among Youth Exposed to Domestic Violence' *Journal of Interpersonal Violence* 16 (9) 944-965

Mitchell MD, Hargrove GL, Collins MH, Thompson MP, Reddick T and Kaslow N (2006) 'Coping Variables that Mediate the Relation between Intimate Partner Violence and Mental Health Outcomes among Low-income, African American women' *Journal of Clinical Psychology* 62 (12) 1503-1520

Moffitt TE and Caspi A (1998) 'Implications of Violence between Intimate Partners for Child Psychologists and Psychiatrists' *Journal of Child Psychology and Psychiatry and Allied Disciplines* 39 (2) 137-144

Moffitt TE and Caspi A (1999) *Findings About Partner Violence from the Dunedin Multidisciplinary Health and Development Study.* (National Institute of Justice, Research in Brief.) Washington: NIJ, US Department of Justice

Moffitt TE and Caspi A (2003) 'Preventing the Intergenerational Continuity of Antisocial Behaviour: Implications of partner violence' in Farrington DP and Coid JW (eds), *Early Prevention of Adult Antisocial Behaviour.* Cambridge: Cambridge University Press

Moyers S, Farmer ERG and Lipscombe JC (2006) 'Contact with Family Members and its Impact on Adolescents and their Foster Placements' *British Journal of Social Work* 36 (4) 541-559

Mullender A (1996) *Rethinking Domestic Violence: The social work and probation response.* London: Routledge

Mullender A, Debbonaire T, Hague G, Kelly L and Malos E (1998) 'Working with Children in Women's Refuges' *Child and Family Social Work* 3 (2) 87-98

Mullender A, Hague G, Iman U, Kelly L, Malos E and Regan L (2002) *Children's Perspectives on Domestic Violence.* London: Sage

Murrell AR, Christoff KA and Henning KR (2007) 'Characteristics of Domestic Violence Offenders: Associations with childhood exposure to violence' *Journal of Family Violence* 22 (7) 523-532

Murrell AR, Merwin RM, Christoff KA and Henning KR (2005) 'When Parents Model Violence: The relationship between witnessing weapon use as a child and later use as an adult' *Behaviour and Social Issues* 14 (2) 128-133

National Council of Juvenile and Family Court Judges (1999) *Effective Intervention in Domestic Violence and Child Maltreatment Cases: Guidelines for policy and practice.* Reno, NV: NCJFCJ

National Offender Management Service Public Protection Unit (2009) *MAPPA Guidance 2009: Version 3.0.* London: Ministry of Justice, National Probation Service, HM Prison Service and ACPO

O'Brien R, Hunt K and Hart G (2005) '"It's Caveman Stuff but that is to a Certain Extent how Guys still Operate": Men's accounts of masculinity and help seeking' *Social Science and Medicine* 61 (3) 503-516

Ofsted (2008) *Safeguarding Children. The third joint chief inspectors' report on arrangements to safeguard children.* London: Ofsted

O'Hagan K and Dillenburger K (1995) *The Abuse of Women within Childcare Work.* Buckingham: Open University Press

O'Leary DA, Barling J, Arias I, Rosenbaum A, Malone J and Tyree A (1989) 'Prevalence and Stability of Physical Aggression between Spouses: A longitudinal analysis' *Journal of Consultant Clinical Psychology* 57 (2) 263-8

Onyskiw JE (2003) 'Domestic Violence and Children's Adjustment' *Journal of Emotional Abuse* 3 (1-2) 11-45

Osborn AL, Delfabbro P and Barber JG (2008) 'The Psychosocial Functioning and Family Background of Children Experiencing Significant Placement Instability in Australian Out-of-home Care' *Children and Youth Services Review* 30 (8) 847-860

Osofsky JD (2003) 'Prevalence of Children's Exposure to Domestic Violence and Child Maltreatment: Implications for prevention and intervention' *Clinical Child and Family Psychology Review* 6 (3) 161-170

Øverlien C (2010) 'Children Exposed to Domestic Violence: Conclusions from the literature and challenges ahead' *Journal of Social Work* 10 (1) 80-97

Øverlien C (2011) 'Abused Women with Children or Children of Abused Women? A study of conflicting perspectives at women's refuges in Norway' *Child and Family Social Work* 16 (1) 71-80

Part D (2006) 'A Flexible Response to Domestic Abuse: Findings from an evaluation' *Practice* 18 (1) 47-58

Peckover S (2003) 'Health Visitors' Understanding of Domestic Violence' *Journal of Advanced Nursing* 44 (2) 200-208

Peled E (1998) 'The Experience of Living with Violence for Preadolescent Children of Battered Women' *Youth and Society* 29 (4) 395-430

Peled E (2000) 'Parenting by Men Who Abuse Women: Issues and dilemmas' *British Journal of Social Work* 30 (1) 25-36

Penell J and Burford G (2000) 'Family Group Decision Making: Protecting children and women' *Child Welfare: Journal of Policy, Practice, and Program* 9 (2) 131-158

Perel G and Peled E (2008) 'The Fathering of Violent Men: Constriction and yearning' *Violence Against Women* 14 (4) 457-482

Piper H and Myers S (2006) 'Forging the Links: (De)constructing chains of behaviours' *Child Abuse Review* 15 (3) 178-187

Pithouse A (2006) 'A Common Assessment for Children in Need? Mixed messages from a pilot study in Wales' *Child Care in Practice* 12 (3) 199-217

Poole A, Beran T and Thurston W (2008) 'Direct and Indirect Services for Children in Domestic Violence Shelters' *Journal of Family Violence* 23 (8) 679-686

Potito C, Day A, Carson E and O'Leary P (2009) 'Domestic Violence and Child Protection: Partnerships and collaboration' *Australian Social Work* 62 (3) 369-387

Povey D (ed) (2004) Crime 2003: Supplementary Volume 1 – *Homicide and gun crime.* London: Home Office

Povey D (ed), Coleman K, Kaiza P and Roe S (2009) *Homicides, Firearm Offences and Intimate Violence 2007/08. (Supplementary Volume 2 to Crime in England and Wales 2007/08.)* (Home Office Statistical Bulletin 02/09.) London: Home Office

Price P, Rajagopalan V and Donaghy P (2009) *Domestic Violence Intervention Project: Improving women and children's safety. Report and evaluation of the East London Domestic Violence Service January 2007-September 2008.* London: DVIP

Protective Behaviours UK (2004), available online at www.protectivebehaviours.co.uk (Accessed 3 September 2010)

Radford L, Blacklock N and Iwi K (2006a) 'Domestic Abuse Assessment and Safety Planning in Child Protection – Assessing perpetrators' in Humphreys C and Stanley N (eds), *Domestic Violence and Child Protection: Directions for good practice.* London: Jessica Kingsley Publishers

Radford L, Corral S, Bradley C, Fisher H, Bassett C and Howat N, with Collishaw S (forthcoming 2011) *The Maltreatment and Victimisation of Children in the UK: NSPCC report on a national survey of young peoples', young adults' and caregivers' experiences.* London: NSPCC

Radford J, Harne L and Trotter J (2006b) 'Disabled Women and Domestic Violence as Violent Crime' Practice: *Social Work in Action* 18 (4) 233-246

Radford L and Hester M (2006) *Mothering through Domestic Violence.* London: Jessica Kingsley Publishers

Radford L, Hester M, Humphries J and Woodfield KS (1997) 'For the Sake of the Children: The law, domestic violence and child contact in England' *Women's Studies International Forum* 20 (4) 471-482

Rakil M (2006) 'Are Men Who Use Violence against their Partners and Children Good Enough Fathers? The need for an integrated child perspective in treatment work with men' in Humphreys C and Stanley N (eds), *Domestic Violence and Child Protection: Directions for good practice.* London: Jessica Kingsley Publishers

Reder P and Duncan S (1999) *Lost Innocents: A follow-up study of fatal child abuse.* London: Routledge

Reder P, Duncan S and Gray M (1993) *Beyond Blame: Child abuse tragedies revisited.* London: Routledge

Reid Howie Associates (2001) *Evaluation of the Zero Tolerance 'Respect' Pilot Project.* Edinburgh: Scottish Executive. Available online at www.scotland.gov.uk/publications/ 2002/06/14934/7698 (Accessed 6 October 2010)

Richards L (2004) *'Getting Away With It': A strategic overview of domestic violence sexual assault and 'serious' incident analysis.* London: Metropolitan Police Service

Richards L, Letchford S and Stratton S (2008) *Policing Domestic Violence.* Oxford: Oxford University Press

Rivett M and Kelly S (2006) 'From Awareness to Practice: Children, domestic violence and child welfare' *Child Abuse Review* 15 (4) 224-242

Robinson A (2004) Domestic Violence MARACS *(Multi-Agency Risk Assessment Conferences) for very High-risk Victims in Cardiff, Wales: A process and outcome evaluation.* Cardiff: Cardiff University

Robinson A (2009) *Independent Domestic Violence Advisors: A process evaluation* Cardiff: Cardiff University

Rose W and Barnes J (2008) *Improving Safeguarding Practice: Study of Serious Case Reviews 2001-2003.* (Research Report DCSF-RR022.) Nottingham: Department for Children Schools and Families

Rosen D, Seng JS, Tolman RM and Mallinger G (2007) 'Intimate Partner Violence, Depression, and Posttraumatic Stress Disorder as Additional Predictors of Low Birth Weight Infants among Low-income Mothers' *Journal of Interpersonal Violence* 22 (10) 1305-1314

Rossman BBR (2000) 'Time Heals All: How much and for whom' *Journal of Emotional Abuse* 2 (1) 31-50

Roustit C, Renahy E, Guernec G, Lesieur S, Parizot I and Chauvin P (2009) 'Exposure to Interparental Violence and Psychosocial Maladjustment in the Adult Life Course: Advocacy for early prevention' *Journal of Epidemiology and Community Health* 63 (7) 563-568

Russell D, Springe KW and Greenfield E (2010) 'Witnessing Domestic Abuse in Childhood as an Independent Risk Factor for Depressive Symptoms in Young Adulthood' *Child Abuse and Neglect* 34 (6) 448-453

Rutter M (1985) 'Resilience in the Face of Adversity: Protective factors and resistance to psychiatric disorder' *British Journal of Psychiatry* 147 (6) 598-611

Rutter M (1989) 'Intergenerational Continuities and Discontinuities in Serious Parenting Difficulties' in Cicchetti D and Carlson V (eds), *Child Maltreatment: Theory and research on the causes and consequences of child abuse and neglect.* Cambridge: Cambridge University Press

Salisbury EJ, Henning K and Holdford R (2009) 'Fathering by Partner-Abusive Men: Attitudes on children's exposure to interparental conflict and risk factors for child abuse' *Child Maltreatment* 14 (3) 232-242

Saltzman KM, Holden GW and Holahan CJ (2005) 'The Psychobiology of Children Exposed to Marital Violence' *Journal of Clinical Child and Adolescent Psychology* 34 (1) 129–139

Sandwell Against Domestic Violence Project (2000) *Violence Free Relationships: Asserting rights. A programme for young people.* Sandwell: SADVP

Sarkar NN (2008) 'The Impact of Intimate Partner Violence on Women's Reproductive Health and Pregnancy Outcome' *Journal of Obstetrics and Gynaecology* 28 (3) 266-271

Sartin RM, Hansen DJ, Huss MT (2006) 'Domestic Violence Treatment Response and Recidivism: A review and implications for the study of family violence' *Aggression and Violent Behavior* 11 (5) 425-40

Saunders A, with Epstein C, Keep G and Debonnaire T (1995) It Hurts Me Too: *Children's experiences of domestic violence and refuge life.* Bristol: Women's Aid Federation of England, ChildLine, and National Institute for Social Work

Saunders H (2004) *Twenty-nine Child Homicides: Lessons still to be learnt on domestic violence and child protection.* Bristol: Women's Aid Federation of England

Schnurr M and Lohmann B (2008) 'How Much Does School Matter? An examination of adolescent dating violence perpetration' *Journal of Youth and Adolescence* 37 (3) 266-283

Scott KL and Crooks CV (2007) 'Preliminary Evaluation of an Intervention Program for Maltreating Fathers' *Brief Treatment and Crisis Intervention* 7 (3) 224-238

Scourfield J (2003) *Gender and Child Protection.* Basingstoke: Palgrave Macmillan

Shepard MF and Pence EL (eds) (1999) *Coordinating Community Responses to Domestic Violence: Lessons from Duluth and beyond.* Thousand Oaks, CA: Sage

Sheppard M (1997) 'Double Jeopardy: The link between child abuse and maternal depression in child and family social work' *Child and Family Social Work* 2 (2) 91-107

Shetty S and Edleson JL (2005) 'Adult Domestic Violence in Cases of International Parental Child Abduction' *Violence Against Women* 11 (1) 89-114

Silovsky JF and Niec L (2002) 'Characteristics of Young Children with Sexual Behavior Problems: A pilot study' *Child Maltreatment* 7 (3) 187-197

Silverman JG, Raj A, Mucci LA and Hathaway JE (2001) 'Dating Violence against Adolescent Girls and Associated Substance Use, Unhealthy Weight Control, Sexual Risk Behaviour, Pregnancy, and Suicidality' *Journal of the American Medical Association* 286 (5) 572–579

Silvern L, Karyl J, Waelde L, Hodges WF, Starek J, Heidt E and Min K (1995) 'Retrospective Reports of Parental Partner Abuse: Relationships to depression, trauma symptoms and self-esteem among college students' *Journal of Family Violence* 10 (2) 177-202

Simonelli CJ, Mullis T, Elliot AN and Pierce TH (2002) 'Abuse by Siblings and Subsequent Experiences of Violence within the Dating Relationship' *Journal of Interpersonal Violence* 17 (2) 103-121

Sinclair R and Bullock R (2002) *Learning from Past Experience: A review of serious case reviews.* London: Department of Health

Sobsey D (2000) 'Faces of Violence against Women with Developmental Disabilities' *Impact* 13 (3) 2-27

Social Services Inspectorate of Wales (2004) *Children in Need – The local authority response to the Victoria Climbié Inquiry: Overview report.* Cardiff: SSIW

Song L, Singer MI and Anglin TM (1998) 'Violence Exposure and Emotional Trauma as Contributors to Adolescents' Violent Behaviors' *Archives of Pediatrics and Adolescent Medicine* 152 (6) 531–536

Spilsbury JC, Kahana S, Drotar D, Creeden R, Flannery D and Friedman S (2008) 'Profiles of Behavioral Problems in Children Who Witness Domestic Violence' *Violence and Victims* 23 (1) 3-17

Stafford A, Stead J and Grimes M (2007) *The Support Needs of Children and Young People who Have to Move Home because of Domestic Abuse.* Edinburgh: Scottish Women's Aid

Stalford H, Baker H and Beveridge F (2003) *Children and Domestic Violence in Rural Areas: A child-focused assessment of service provision*. London: Save the Children

Stanko E (2001) 'The Day to Count: Reflections on a methodology to raise awareness about the impact of domestic violence in the UK' *Criminology and Criminal Justice* 1 (2) 215-226

Stanko E, Crisp D, Hale C and Lucraft H (1998) *Counting the Costs: Estimating the impact of domestic violence in the London Borough of Hackney*. Swindon: Crime Concern

Stanley N (1997) 'Domestic Violence and Child Abuse: Developing social work practice' *Child and Family Social Work* 2 (3) 135-145

Stanley N, Ellis J and Bell J (2010a) 'Delivering Preventive Programmes in Schools: Identifying gender issues' in Barter C and Berridge D (eds), *Children Behaving Badly? Exploring peer violence between children and young people*. Chichester: Wiley

Stanley N, Fell B, Miller P, Thomson G and Watson J (2009) *Men's Talk: Research to inform Hull's social marketing initiative on domestic violence*. Preston: University of Central Lancashire

Stanley N and Humphreys C (2006) 'Multi-Agency and Multi-Disciplinary Work: Barriers and opportunities' in Humphreys C and Stanley N (eds), *Domestic Violence and Child Protection: Directions for good practice*. London: Jessica Kingsley Publishers

Stanley N, Miller P, Richardson Foster H and Thomson G (2010b) 'A Stop-start Response: Social services' interventions with children and families notified during domestic violence incidents' *British Journal of Social Work*, online advance access available from http://bjsw.oxfordjournals.org/content/early/2010/06/19/bjsw.bcq071 (Accessed 10 October 2010)

Stanley N, Miller P, Richardson Foster H and Thomson G (2010c) *Children and Families Experiencing Domestic Violence: Police and children's social services' responses*. London: NSPCC. Available online at www.nspcc.org.uk/Inform/research/findings/children_experiencing_domestic_violence_report_wdf70355.pdf (Accessed 2 September 2010)

Stanley N, Miller P, Richardson Foster H and Thomson G (2010d) 'Children's Experiences of Domestic Violence: Developing an integrated response from police and child protection services' *Journal of Interpersonal Violence* first published on 1.10.10 as doi:10.1177/0886260510383030

Statham J (2004) 'Effective Services to Support Children in Special Circumstances' *Child Care, Health and Development* 30 (6) 589-598

Sterne A and Poole L with Chadwick D, Lawler C and Dodd LW (2010) *Domestic Violence and Children: A handbook for schools and early years settings*. London: Routledge

Stith SM, Smith DB, Penn CE, Ward DB and Tritt D 2004 'Intimate Partner Physical Abuse Perpetration and Victimization Risk Factors: A meta-analytic review' *Aggression and Violent Behavior* 10 (1) 65-98

Stover CS, Van Horn P, Turner R, Cooper B and Lieberman AF (2003) 'The Effects of Father Visitation on Preschool-Aged Witnesses of Domestic Violence' *Journal of Interpersonal Violence* 18 (10) 1149-1166

Straus M, Gelles RJ and Steinmetz SK (1980) *Behind Closed Doors: Violence in the American family*. Newbury Park, CA: Sage

Sturge C and Glaser D (2000) 'Contact and Domestic Violence: The experts' court report' *Family Law* 30 (September) 615-628

Sullivan CM and Bybee DM (1999) 'Reducing Violence Using Community-based Advocacy for Women with Abusive Partners' *Journal of Consulting and Clinical Psychology* 67 (1) 43-53

Sullivan CM, Nguyen H, Allen N, Bybee D and Juras J (2000) 'Beyond Searching for Deficits: Evidence that physically and emotionally abused women are nurturing parents' *Journal of Emotional Abuse* 2 (1) 51-71

Sullivan PM and Knutson JF (2000) 'Maltreatment and Disabilities: A population-based epidemiological study' *Child Abuse and Neglect* 24 (10) 1257-1273

Taft A, Watson L and Lee C (2004) 'Violence Against Young Australian Women and Association with Reproductive Events: A cross-sectional analysis of a national population sample' *The Australian and New Zealand Journal of Public Health* 28 (4) 324-329

Tallieu TL and Brownridge DA (2010) 'Violence against Pregnant Women: Prevalence, patterns, risk factors, theories, and directions for future research' *Aggression and Violent Behavior* 15 (1) 14-35

Teicher M (2002) 'Scars That Won't Heal: The neurobiology of child abuse' *Scientific American* 286 (3) 70

Testa M, Livingston JA and Leonard KE (2003) 'Women's Substance Use and Experiences of Intimate Partner Violence: A longitudinal investigation among a community sample' *Addictive Behaviors* 28 (9) 1649-1664

The Scottish Government (2010) *The Caledonian System*, available online at www.scotland.gov.uk/Topics/People/Equality/violence-women/CaledonianSystem (Accessed 10 October 2010)

Thiara R and Chung D (2008) *Domestic Violence and Abuse Notifications Screening Pilot: An evaluation.* (Unpublished report.) Warwick: University of Warwick

Thiara RK (2010) 'Continuing Control: Child contact and post-separation violence' in Thiara RK and Gill AK (eds), *Violence Against Women in South Asian Communities: Issues for policy and practice.* London: Jessica Kingsley Publishers

Tyndall-Lind A, Landreth GL and Giordano MA (2001) 'Intensive Group Play Therapy with Child Witnesses of Domestic Violence' *International Journal of Play Therapy* 10 (1) 53-83

Velleman R, Templeton L, Reuber D, Klein M and Moesgen D (2008) 'Domestic Abuse Experienced by Young People Living in Families with Alcohol Problems: Results from a cross-European study' *Child Abuse Review* 17 (6) 387-409

Walby S (2004) *The Cost of Domestic Violence.* London: Department of Trade and Industry

Walby S (2009) *The Cost of Domestic Violence: Up-date 2009.* Lancaster: Lancaster University Available online at www.lancs.ac.uk/fass/doc_library/sociology/Cost_of_domestic_violence_update.doc (Accessed 25 January 2011)

Walby S and Allen J (2004) *Domestic Violence, Sexual Assault and Stalking: Findings from the British Crime Survey.* (Home Office Research Study 276.) London: Home Office Research, Development and Statistics Directorate

Walker A, Flatley J, Kershaw C and Moon D (eds) (2009) *Crime in England and Wales 2008/09. Volume 1: Findings from the British Crime Survey and police recorded crime.* (Home Office Statistical Bulletin 11/09 Volume 1.) London: Home Office

Wathen CN and MacMillan H (2003) 'Interventions for Violence against Women: Scientific review' *Journal of American Medical Association* 89 (5) 589-600

Watson D and Parsons S (2005) *Domestic Abuse of Women and Men in Ireland: Report on the national study of domestic abuse.* Dublin: National Crime Council

Webb E, Shankleman J, Evans MR and Brooks R (2001) 'The Health of Children in Refuges for Women Victims of Domestic Violence: Cross sectional descriptive survey' *British Medical Journal* 323 (7306) 210-213

Wekerle C, Leung E, Wall A, MacMillan H, Boyle M, Trocme N and Waechter R (2009) 'The Contribution of Childhood Emotional Abuse to Teen Dating Violence among Child Protective Services-Involved Youth' *Child Abuse and Neglect* 33 (1) 45-58

Wekerle C and Wolfe DA (1999) 'Dating Violence in Mid-adolescence: Theory, significance, and emerging prevention initiatives' *Clinical Psychology Review* 19 (4) 435-456

Wellock VK (2010) 'Domestic Abuse: Black and minority-ethnic women's perspectives' *Midwifery* 26 (2) 181-188

Welsh K (2008) 'Partnership or Palming Off? Involvement in partnership initiatives on domestic violence' *Howard Journal of Criminal Justice* 47 (2) 170-188

Westcott HL, Jones DP (1999) 'The Abuse of Disabled Children' *Journal of Child Psychology and Psychiatry* 40 (4) 497-506

Whitaker D, Morrison S, Lindquist C, Hawkins S, O'Neil J, Nesius A, Mathew A and Reese L (2006) 'A Critical Review of Interventions for the Primary Prevention of Perpetration of Partner Violence' *Aggression and Violent Behavior* 11 (2) 151-166

White A, Fawkner HJ and Holmes M (2006) 'Is there a Case for Differential Treatment of Young Men and Women?' *Medical Journal of Australia* 185 (8) 454-455

White AK and Johnson M (2000) 'Men Making Sense of their Chest Pain – Niggles, doubts and denials' *Journal of Clinical Nursing* 9 (4) 534-541

White C, Warrener M, Reeves A and La Valle I (2008) *Family Intervention Projects: An Evaluation of their design, set-up and early outcomes.* (Research Report No DCSF-RW047.) London: DCSF. Available online at http://education.gov.uk/publications/eOrderingDownload/DCSF-RW047.pdf (Accessed 30 January 2011)

Whitfield CL, Anda RF, Dube SR and Felitti VJ (2003) 'Violent Childhood Experiences and the Risk of Intimate Partner Violence in Adults' *Journal of Interpersonal Violence* 18 (2) 166-185

Williamson E and Abrahams H (2010) *Evaluation of the Bristol Freedom Programme.* Bristol: University of Bristol

Williamson E and Hester M (2009) *Evaluation of the South Tyneside Domestic Abuse Perpetrator Programme 2006-2008: Final report.* Bristol: University of Bristol. Available online at www.bristol.ac.uk/sps/research/projects/completed/2009/rl6866/finalreport.pdf (Accessed 30 January 2011)

Wilson A (2010) 'Charting South Asian Women's Struggles against Gender-based Violence' in Thiara RK and Gill AK (eds), *Violence Against Women in South Asian Communities: Issues for policy and practice.* London: Jessica Kingsley Publishers

Wolak J and Finkelhor D (1998) "Effects of Partner Violence on Children' in Jasinski JL and Williams LM (eds), *Partner Violence: A comprehensive review of 20 years of research.* Thousand Oaks, CA: Sage

Wolfe DA, Crooks CV, Lee V, McIntyre-Smith A and Jaffe PG (2003) 'The Effects of Children's Exposure to Domestic Violence: A meta-analysis and critique' *Clinical Child and Family Psychology Review* 6 (3) 171-187

Wolfe DA and Jaffe PG (1999) 'Emerging Strategies in the Prevention of Domestic Violence' *The Future of Children* 9 (3) 133-144

Wood M, Barter C and Berridge D (forthcoming 2011) *'It's Just Me, Standing on My Own Two Feet': Disadvantaged teenagers, intimate partner violence and coercive control.* London: NSPCC

Yoshihama M and Mills LG (2003) 'When is the Personal Professional in Child Welfare Practice? The influence of intimate partner and child abuse histories on workers in domestic violence cases' *Child Abuse and Neglect* 27 (3) 319-336

Zerk DM and Mertin PG (2009) 'Domestic Violence and Maternal Reports of Young Children's Functioning' *Journal of Family Violence* 24 (7) 423-432

Index

About the author

Nicky Stanley
Professor of Social Work at the University of Central Lancashire

Nicky Stanley is well-known for her research in the areas of child welfare and safeguarding, domestic violence, children's and young people's mental health, and interprofessional work. Recent research commissions have included a national evaluation of social work practice pilot projects and an evaluation of a social marketing campaign and service for male perpetrators of domestic violence. She has co-edited books on domestic violence and child protection, inquiries in health and social care, students' mental health needs and institutional abuse. She has authored a book on mothers' mental health needs and child protection and publishes widely in a range of academic and professional journals. She is co-editor of *Child Abuse Review*. A trained social worker, Nicky practised in a range of settings with both children and adults in England and Scotland before moving into education and training of practitioners.

About research in practice

research in practice has been working with its Partner agencies to promote evidence-informed practice since 1996. Our mission is to build the capacity for evidence-informed practice in children's services. Our work brings together practitioner expertise with formal research evidence – creating new knowledge, new skills and a new energy to improve outcomes for children, young people and their families.

research in practice is a department of The Dartington Hall Trust run in collaboration with the University of Sheffield. The Dartington Hall Trust is a pioneering charity - a place of experiment, enterprise, and education where the arts, social justice and sustainability come together.

Other titles in this series of research in practice research reviews include:

Information about these and the full range of research in practice publications is available online.

www.rip.org.uk/publications